THE 4 FACETS
OF GRIEF

THE 4 FACETS OF GRIEF

HEAL YOUR HEART,
REBUILD YOUR WORLD,
AND FIND NEW PATHWAYS TO JOY

By
Ruth E. Field, LCSW

ISBN 10: 0-9990862-0-0
ISBN 13: 978-0-9990862-0-9

Praise for
The 4 Facets of Grief

★★★★★**One of the best books I've read on grief!**

"One of the best books I've read on grief. Ruth gives concrete steps and tips to facilitate the grieving process. With an understanding that comes from personal, painful experience, she manages to step into the grief process and shine a light at the end of the tunnel. It is clearly Ruth's calling to help others through the grief process and to come out stronger on the other side, and she does so in this wonderful book!"

~ Denise K. Ambre, LCSW

★★★★★**A generous and wise guide for times of loss**

"Pull up a chair and allow Ruth Field to guide you through the most difficult time of your life as only a woman who has gone through her own deep healing can. Following the sudden death of her son, the author found ways to be resilient, find meaning, and stay connected, always honoring herself and her son's life, which she cherished but lost.

In The 4 Facets of Grief, she generously shares her wisdom, experience and expertise as a mother, professional grief counselor, and guide. In your most vulnerable time it is natural to wonder, 'How will I ever get through this?' Ruth Field and The 4 Facets of Grief will point the way."

~ Analesa Berg, Transformational
Artist, Spiritual Counselor

★ ★ ★ ★ ★ **Hope......,**

"I will be keeping this book within reach for years to come. The tools that the author provides us with to deal with grief spill over into other areas of my life. She convinces me that I can not only get through losses and unwelcome life changes that feel overwhelming, but grow from them. The author's own ability to move forward positively in spite of devastating losses inspires me and I feel empowered by the clear, simple exercises I can start right NOW to move forward. This book delivers a message of acceptance and adaptation.... a message of hope. Life's losses are inevitable, but how we handle them is our choice."

~ Carola Carren

★★★★★The Only Grief Book You Need to Understand Your Grief

"As a clinical therapist, I often discuss with clients the 5 stages of grief we have all heard of (denial, anger, bargaining, depression and acceptance), but oftentimes it was just not a good fit/description. I found one I like a whole lot better in this book. Ruth Field's discussion of grief (Accepting, Adapting, Meaning Making, Replenishing and Synthesizing) is more relatable. I found myself thinking of not only clients, but of myself and loved ones who have experienced grief. I was nodding along, and really appreciating how she put my own feelings into words. I also liked how she encourages us to think even deeper with her questions to generate relatable experiences and making meaning of our feelings. I will not only be using this book in my practice, but sharing it with loved ones for years to come. I am grateful for this book."

~ dltd

★★★★★Will heal many hearts for years to come

"In The Four Facets of Grief the reader is gently guided along the path to healing from the devastating loss of a loved one. The principles to guide this journey were developed through the author's grief counseling practice, research, and experience of multiple personal losses, including the tragic death of her son. Ruth Field knows first-hand that healing a grieving heart is hard work, and that "you don't move on from your loss; you are always moving through it in evolving ways." With warmth and wisdom, she offers those who are grieving a source of practical help, hope, and inspiration."

~ Judy Dressner, OTD, OTR/L

Doctor of Occupational Therapy, Licensed Occupational Therapist

Adjunct Professor, M.S. in Applied Gerontology

The College of Health Sciences, Brenau University

★★★★★ This is not a sad book; it is a book of hope.

"A well-written account on meaning-making about the one thing all of us must eventually face: death. This is not a sad book; it is a book of hope. Not a subject one would normally willingly embrace, but this book leaves one with empathy and better understanding. I find two concepts immensely helpful: The author helps one understand that it is OK to grief in a way that makes sense to you and secondly how to create meaning-making that resonates with who you are and your belief system. In my counseling practice, I deal with many problems arising from unresolved grief, and I applaud those who embrace the process and help others to process through all the stages in a meaningful way. A book I will highly recommend."

~ Louise VN Liebenberg

★ ★ ★ ★ ★ **Wisdom in Grief.**

"With words of hope, Ruth E Field writes 'Through it all [grief] remember that you are a beautiful, precious, and unrepeatable miracle who deserves to be happy.' This wonderful book helps to comfort and sustain us through grieving. Grief is not a popular topic, yet each of us will experience grief in our lifetimes. Ruth E Field courageously shares her grief with us, revisiting the pain of the loss of her son so we, her readers can be helped. She writes 'This was my ending of life as I knew it … Agony, agony.'

She speaks later in the book, 'I learned that most bereaved parents have some version of this need to know their child is okay, somewhere, and that the love they shared will somehow continue. That's powerful motivation to open up one's ideas about what's possible. With my passion thus normalized, I carried on in earnest.' Please read this book if it is for you or share it with anyone you know who would benefit from the empathy and wisdom of this author."

~ Dr. Denise A Nisbet, Clinical Psychologist (retired)

★ ★ ★ ★ ★ **I could not put this book down!**

"I could not put this book down! A trained grief counselor, Field knows what she is talking about both from her professional experience helping others as well as her personal life. In The 4 FACETS OF GRIEF, she takes us through the various feelings that losing a child (or any horrific event) creates and how to cope with those feelings. Intertwined is her personal story about the tragic loss of her own son. More than a textbook, this book offers a sensitive yet realistic way to face forward after tragedy and not only survive, but thrive."

~ Laura Temkin

★★★★★Excellent book for professionals and anyone experiencing the rawness of grief.

"Ms. Field writes from vast professional experience as well as from her own experience of grief and loss. The author through years of experience has taken time-tested information about grief-- such as normal grief, stages of grief, mourning, etc. and weaves this material into a brilliant NEW concept that she designed and developed.

Grief is part of being human and Ms. Field provides the tools and the hope to heal, rebuild, and find the joy in your heart once again. This book is part memoir and part self-help guide. She provides a remarkable system to reclaim your humanness as a partner in life.

Extremely refreshing in her approach to navigate through the forest of grief and loss. I highly recommend this book."

~ Wendy Van de Poll, MS, CEOL - Center For Pet Loss Grief

★★★★★ **Helpful, Logical Read**

"Having navigated sudden and unexpected losses in the past, this book was comforting to me to see what I did right! Beautifully written, it guides you through aspects of grieving, whether they be life alterations, or deaths, and for me, gave many more coping tips that I anticipate needing in the future."

~ Nancy Winn, RN, BSN
Critical Care Nursing (retired)

Disclaimer

This book is not meant to replace the advice and counsel of your personal healthcare provider and is for educational purposes only. If you ever feel you can no longer function in life, have suicidal thoughts, or if any of the normal grief feelings become extreme, you may have developed complicated grief. Please call your hospital, medical practitioner, therapist, or other mental health professional for help right away.

Dedication

In loving memory of David E. Field

October 25, 1984 – July 24, 2011

My son, my teacher, and forever

The boy with the beautiful heart.

Table of Contents

Acknowledgments

There were so many wonderful people who inspired me to write this book and helped me to realize a long-held dream! I appreciate all the patience and encouragement from family, friends, and colleagues.

To Alan: thank you for bringing light into the darkness.

To Lisa and Andy, Erika and Adam, Stephanie and Noah: thank you for inspiring me to keep going. You work so hard, give so much, and love so passionately!

To Emily, Tyler, Julia, Joshua, Aaron, Rose, Ariel, and grandchildren not yet born: thank you for being living proof of joy, hope, wonder, and discovery! I cherish every moment as your Bubbe.

To Chandler Bolt, Sean Sumner, and the entire SPS staff and Mastermind Community, thank you for the structure, wisdom, and unflagging support throughout this process. Special appreciation goes to Judy Dressner, my steadfast accountability partner and cherished friend!

I also want to express my gratitude to My Tribe of fellow grievers, and my dear clients who trust me with your deepest thoughts and feelings. This book would not be possible if you had not been willing to share your journeys with me. I am deeply honored.

The 4 Facets Grief – Introduction

"**H**ow am I going to go on?"
"When will this pain end?"

"Will I ever stop crying?"

These are questions I am asked most often when people begin grief counseling. They are feeling lost and in agony with no clear path to healing relief, for the reality of death is all consuming and inarguably final.

Losing someone you love is a devastating experience. It is excruciatingly painful and hard to wrap your mind around. Trying to understand how this could have happened and then figuring out how to move forward can leave you overwhelmed, suffering, heartbroken, and frightened. It happens to everyone sooner or later, and most of us have to face it many times in our lives.

We know the human response to loss is grief, but we don't know exactly how to deal with it. Did you ever take a course in school called Grieving 101? Did your parents ever sit you down for The Grief Talk? Probably not.

The subjects of death, grief, and loss make most of us uncomfortable because there are no quick fixes. Nothing anyone can say will bring your loved one back or take away the pain. No amount of support will suddenly bring about relief. And because it feels impossible to accept the unacceptable, we learn by osmosis to put misery on the back burner and pretend we're mostly okay.

But we're not okay; this is not business as usual. We're left with that burning question: "How do I go on?"

This very question inspired the book you are about to read.

Ever since I can remember, I've struggled with life and death questions. What does it all mean? How does the universe work? Why am I here? It's partly just who I am and partly due to life's circumstances.

You see, in addition to my training and experience as a clinical social worker, I also have a lifetime of practice managing my own journeys of grief. The most difficult of these has been the death of my son. Along the way, I noted what has helped and hindered me, my family, and my clients in our universal quest to move through life's most difficult times. Like my clients, I didn't want to just survive these ordeals; I wanted to ultimately thrive.

I believe the answer to our existential questions lies in developing habits that enhance grief resilience – the ability to move through unwelcome change and achieve a sense of wellness and peace. Many people believe you either *are* resilient or you're not; as if it were a personality trait. I believe grief resilience is actually a skill set that can be learned, practiced, and incorporated into your life.

By combining the insights and understanding gleaned from the long-term study of myself and others, I developed a system that builds grief resilience and moves the reader from heartache to healing. It is hard work, but it does promote wellness and growth.

The 4 Facets of Grief details four different aspects of enhancing your coping capacity with examples and skill-building ideas relating to each one. Using a GPS analogy, it provides a road map for navigating your personal reality, recognizing that you are in the driver's seat. You get to choose when to push onward and when to take a break; which stops need more focus, and which stops are quick visits. You even get to choose your route and circle back to particular points more than once. Every journey will be unique and according to your needs at the time.

Another analogy, and the one that inspired the name of this book, is that of creating a gemstone out of the earth's raw materials. The stone begins as a mostly unappealing rock or crystals with varying chemical compositions. Through an exacting technique of cutting, polishing, and refining, the stone's brilliance and luster are revealed. That rough hunk of minerals is now a unique creation of beauty and joy.

If you've ever wished you felt more confident about navigating loss, this book will show you exactly how to proceed. Using the system described here, my clients are already building new serenity to get through their own worst-case scenarios, having been challenged to accept the loss of loved ones from illness, accident, suicide, and other tragic events. And having tested every tip on myself as well, I am certain this is a user-friendly approach to wellbeing.

I have been honored over the years to hear that grief resilience training has indeed helped my clients. Bereaved parents say they don't know how families get through such heartbreak without learning these skills. Spouses who incorporate grief resilience training through the final days of their loved one's illness and beyond are grateful for its benefit. And grieving siblings report moving from shock and trauma to peace and compassion.

If you follow the skill-building guide in this book, you will feel more resilient, utilize better coping strategies, and create greater serenity than you ever thought possible. You will notice your relationships improving as you move through sorrow and reintegrate peace and even joy. And you'll increase your self-confidence, realizing that if you can get through this, you can probably get through anything.

You already know how devastating it is to have the rug pulled out from under you. You don't have to be the person who lays there in pain indefinitely. Be the one who acknowledges the reality of loss and plans how to thoughtfully respond. There will be bruises to heal, new thoughts and feelings to understand, and different meanings to consider. And through it all, you'll be creating your own personal self-care practice that keeps you replenished and able to get up and go on.

Don't wait one more minute to start feeling and functioning like the person you know you were meant to be.

The grief resilience system you are about to learn creates meaningful and sustainable results. Each chapter provides new insights and actions that will make a positive difference to your ability to go forward.

I'm excited and honored to be your companion on this journey of renewal, as we hone your natural resources to form a radiant new you. Let's get started!

Endings and Beginnings

"All transitions begin with endings. Endings must precede new beginnings and yet many, immobilized by an understandable fear, will refuse this call, recoil from this adventure and grasp onto the old ways, losing personal power, creativity, and life force."

~ Elliott S. Dacher, MD, *Transitions: A Guide to the 6 Stages of a Life Transition*

I used to think life was a series of beginnings. Birth is a beginning; starting school is a beginning. So is learning to drive; new love; a new home. All these firsts take us toward presumably better and more fulfilling experiences. Beginnings are filled with hope, promise, and expectation. Sometimes they're exhilarating and scary in the most positive way. But I honestly didn't consider the possibility that they also may follow endings. At least, not until I became intimately acquainted with loss.

I eventually realized that endings must precede new beginnings. In every instance I could think of, new adventures signaled the end of something that was there before. The birth of a baby is the end of pregnancy, for instance. Many times we're thrilled for a situation to be ending; we're ready to move on. Then there are other moments of painful loss when the ending just feels impossibly wrong.

This is unwelcome change. It's human nature to seek the familiar, and whether we realize it or not, we all have this tendency. It's comforting to be in familiar territory – physically, emotionally, and spiritually. Navigating any change can be challenging, but being thrust into unwelcome change is moving into a bleak unknown.

Becoming a Bereaved Mother

My son's death has been such an unwelcome change for me. The ending of his life was the beginning of mine as a bereaved mother. And even though I had already experienced the deaths of many people close to me, this was unmistakably different. It felt as if I was in a nightmarish club no one would ever want to join, and I couldn't get out. It felt impossible.

I was heartbroken, scared, and totally unsure how to proceed. In fact, I could not even imagine proceeding at all. I was also angry, sad, and thinking life was completely unfair; longing to return to a time before the accident happened. I imagined life was simpler then, and I wanted that back. I actually fantasized about time going backward so I could have a "do-over" with a different outcome. But since that wasn't possible, I was left to somehow cope with circumstances I never imagined for myself. I definitely did not sign up for *this*.

Slowly (almost imperceptibly slowly), I began surrendering to the process of change. I allowed myself to really feel the loss and the pain it created. I learned to regulate how and when to let in the pain so I could feel some measure of control. There were eventually days in which I didn't think deeply about my son's accident and death at all; then there were other moments when I was overcome with agony and tears.

Slow surrender is not the same as denial, in which we act as if the loss has not happened at all. It's an accumulation of alternating moments in which we expose ourselves to the inevitable reality of current life and distract ourselves from it, all the while feeling whatever there is to feel.

Ultimately, I began to reconnect with myself. After a long time, my sense of who I am came together again, and I began to feel grounded in my reality. What happened to our family became old news and that sinking feeling in the pit of my stomach upon awakening each morning was finally gone. To be sure, there are still pangs of sorrow, and there always will be, but I no longer feel lost in a strange land. I know who I am and what happened, and I know I'll ultimately be okay ... albeit in a very different way.

I've been told I'm resilient. To be honest, I don't really feel that way, if resilient means being sure, I can easily handle anything life dishes out. Some people equate resilience with strength, and although I think of it as *a* strength, I don't believe feeling strong is the only route to resilience. I actually believe we access our strength through our vulnerability.

What I'm experiencing now is an acknowledgment that I've endured some traumatic and distressing times and that I'm still here, breathing, working, loving, and living the best I can. Some moments are still painful, some are okay, and there are even times of joy and laughter, which I doubted would ever be possible early on in my grief.

Overall, I think I'm living with my son's death as well as can be expected considering how it happened and how much I miss him. But it has been a slow process of discovery that has brought me to the point at which I can write about my experience.

So what does resilient mean? One dictionary definition includes, "being able to recover quickly from setbacks" and "being able to spring back quickly into shape after being bent, stretched, or squashed."

Although I can't imagine anyone *quickly* bouncing back from suffering loss, it does make sense to work toward recovering one's emotional, physical, and spiritual "shape" in the aftermath. I know I definitely felt bent, stretched, and squashed. I also felt ripped open, turned inside out, and shattered.

After a long time, I have arrived at a new sense of self. My life-transition of loss is now inseparable from who I am, and I am able to consider how I might use this reality to make my life even more meaningful than ever before.

To begin learning grief resilience, we must acknowledge the existence of unwelcome change. We may not like the endings we endure, but they always lead to new beginnings. Here is the story of my own losses of loved ones and what I've learned through the ongoing process.

Recollections of Loss

"Are you Ruth Field?" asked one of the three grim-faced officers who appeared at my door that Sunday night.

"Are you the mother of David Field?" he clarified.

"Yes," came my robot-like answer as time slowed and reality splintered crazily. The officer took my trembling hand in his and pronounced a script I will never forget.

"This evening, David was involved in a very serious accident, and his injuries were so severe that he was not able to survive. I'm so sorry for your loss."

This was my ending – of life as I knew it. Somehow, I had to understand that my handsome, smart, successful, beloved 26-year-old son had stopped living in the last few hours. I remember screaming "NO!" and losing the ability to stand. All I could do at that moment was say no to everything as my world seemed to collapse around me.

Agony, agony. I was in shock and disbelief; I couldn't wrap my mind around any information. I could not understand simple sentences or know what to do next. Functioning in any kind of reasonable way was impossible. Looking at my surroundings produced wild distortions like mirrors in a carnival fun-house.

Thinking back to that night makes me realize how far I've come in living with my grief, and I'm grateful to be in this moment. I'm also aware that my entire life has provided a multitude of opportunities for me to learn about grieving.

By the time of my son's death, I had already learned there is a big difference between anticipated and sudden loss. My father, mother, sister, best friend, dear neighbor, and cherished colleague all died after lengthy battles against incurable illnesses. I was a caregiver for some; other times my role was visitor, helper, and witness. Watching a loved one in pain is excruciating. No, it's not the same physical pain they're enduring, but an instinctive anguish that permeates the soul.

On visiting days, I didn't want to be there but couldn't stay away. I wished desperately that I (or anyone) could do something to lift them out of their suffering. It became difficult to eat, sleep, and manage my daily tasks. And I prayed for release – theirs and mine. I remember asking the universe repeatedly for their freedom from suffering, all the while knowing it would mean a permanent loss for me. Part of me yearned to get back to life as it had been, and part of me didn't want to face a world without my loved ones.

I wanted each of them to be free from pain and at peace, and I also wanted their ongoing presence in my life. I struggled with guilt for the relief that came with death, and I would also have given anything for their complete recovery. Such opposing emotions and thoughts! All are compelling at the same time.

My brother-in-law, my nephew, and my son all died young (but many years apart) after tragic accidents.

While it's true that we were all spared the agony of long-term illness related misery, the shock that came with the news of their deaths was equally debilitating. There is an unbelievable quality to news of death like this; you just can't quite absorb it. I remember asking the same questions over and over, as if somehow, the answers would change, or it would start to make sense.

Time slowed, and I felt like I'd been punched in the stomach and had the wind knocked out of me. Everything felt surreal and distant in those early days of shock, which delayed the beginning of active grieving in an important and necessary way.

In each instance, we were told my dear ones knew no suffering. They were killed instantly, and for that, I felt grateful. But oh the pain and guilt around what wasn't said! If only I had known our time was limited, I would have said and done things so differently! And wondering about their last moments – last thoughts; last feelings – created more waves of torment.

Losing a loved one through lengthy illness or sudden death is traumatic no matter how you look at it. Terminal illness allows for some amount of pre-grieving or mental preparation, even though that in no way makes the loss any easier. Sudden death gets it all over with in an instant, even though we're reeling in disbelief and left longing for farewell.

Anticipating a loss does not protect us from the shock of finality, and sudden death does not erase our yearning for closure. Having experienced both kinds of loss, here is what I know for sure: we are never ready to say goodbye to the people we love.

So many endings. The years of loss gave me a very personal view of suffering and death from a variety of perspectives. At one point, I even felt like Typhoid Mary – it seemed as if everyone close to me died, so I must be some kind of disaster carrier. With time and therapy, however, I came to believe I have a sacred duty to bear witness to grief and to support others in their bereavement.

A Different Approach

Inhabiting reality; stepping into the pain. Letting it wash over you, pounding and wounding ... this is the challenge of grief. It's learning to tolerate discomfort, to look heartbreak in the eye and still breathe.

Over 30 years ago, Elizabeth Kubler-Ross famously detailed five stages that have come to be known as the Five Stages of Grief. (Elisabeth Kubler-Ross, *On Death and Dying* (New York: Macmillan, 1969), 45-60.)

They include denial, anger, bargaining, depression, and acceptance. My research indicates she was actually noting what people go through in the process of accepting their own terminal illness and impending death; not necessarily the death of a loved one. However, her framework came to be accepted as the process by which we navigate all grief.

When it comes to mourning the death of loved ones, here is what I've learned. I don't believe our emotions are so predictable and linear that they will fall into any neat structure. Nor do I think anyone ever completes an aspect of grieving with a sense of accomplishment and readiness to tackle the next one.

I don't even believe we are ever finished with the grief process, much to our friends' and families' frustration. Grieving does change and evolve, as do we with time. We weave new truths and understandings into the fabric of our reality, and ultimately, see the entire tapestry as a necessary, meaningful product of those changes. Our losses are thus bound into the backdrop of our lives

Grieving is not meant to help us get over what happened; it allows us to incorporate the loss into the rest of our lives. The experience of grief is as individual as we are, with overlapping and recurring waves. I believe our job is to ride the waves and learn to rest in the calm between them.

My Calling

Loss is unavoidable. Because we are all human, everyone eventually dies. Sooner or later, we will experience the death of someone we love; it's impossible to get through a lifetime without that.

It's much easier to cope with losing someone at the end of their natural lifetime from what seem to be natural causes. Of course, we're sad and never really ready for them to go, but it makes sense in a world that should follow our expectations. As I've said, it's shattering to cope with losing someone prematurely, suddenly, or through terrible suffering. None of these seems fair, and they're not.

But there are also new beginnings that come out of those endings. We may be pushed toward them kicking and screaming all the way, and we still find ourselves having to figure out what to do and how to be in this new environment. It's not an easy task, and I don't think it comes instinctively.

There are no classes called Grief 101 and no instruction manuals distributed by hospitals, nursing homes, funeral homes, etc. Everyone acknowledges grieving is an individual pursuit and we may recognize common feelings, but there is no education telling us how to get from a painful ending to a peaceful new beginning.

This is my calling. The only way I can make any sense of the repeated and varied exposure to loss that life has given me is to dedicate myself to helping others navigate such endings and beginnings and share what I've learned. I am here to be Griefhelper; to help you believe in new beginnings

Losing someone we love is admittedly, completely discombobulating. It's crazy-making and defies any sense of order. It's also human nature to look for and/or create order in the midst of chaos, thereby, making this impossible reality just a little more approachable. Order helps to break down the enormity of loss into more bite-sized chunks, which are, hopefully, a little more digestible.

The Four Facets of Grief

And so, I present in this book a new approach to coping with loss. Instead of trying to identify what stage of grief we're in, always hoping to be "done" with the chore, I propose that there are facets of the experience that are useful in turning endings into beginnings, thereby, building grief resilience. These facets keep us moving forward in the early days of sadness, through years of incorporating it into our lives, and even into decades of memory.

The Four Facets of grief are purposely stated as verbs in the present continuous tense. **Accepting, Adapting,**

Meaning-Making, and Replenishing all convey action that is current and ongoing. There is no point at which we are finished even though we can certainly be aware of progress. Likewise, there is no implied order. Feel free to read and implement the sections as your interest leads you. Because each of us is so individual, some sections may resonate more fully than others; some may grab you, threatening never to let go, while others may seem barely relevant.

Trust your instincts; the sections are there to enhance your thought process. If something doesn't seem important, you may have already started working through that facet or may not be ready yet to do so. Either one is okay.

Another important note is that the facets are not mutually exclusive. You don't finish one before moving on to another. In fact, they overlap and co-occur all the time. You do, however, get to choose which facet you will explore at any given moment. The more you play around with them, the more you will begin to sense how they fit together for you.

Chapter Summary

In this first chapter, you considered the idea of endings leading to beginnings. You learned the story of my son's death as well as the deaths of my other close family members and friends. You now understand my calling to be a Griefhelper and the resulting Four Facets approach to the grieving process.

What's Ahead

In Part One, I'll explore the first facet of grief: **Accepting.** You may be thinking it's not possible to accept the death of someone you love. Join me now for the next chapter's reflection on Accepting the Unacceptable.

PART ONE

Accepting

Accepting the Unacceptable

"You will lose someone you can't live without, and your heart will be badly broken, and the bad news is that you never completely get over the loss of your beloved. But this is also the good news. They live forever in your broken heart that doesn't seal back up. And you come through. It's like having a broken leg that never heals perfectly – that still hurts when the weather gets cold, but you learn to dance with the limp."

~ Anne Lamott

Why is it so difficult to accept unwelcome change? And how can we possibly accept circumstances that feel unacceptable? Join me in this chapter's exploration of what it means to accept and how you might begin the process.

Defining Acceptance

The first step is to figure out what acceptance really means. According to the Merriam-Webster dictionary, acceptance is the quality or state of being accepted or acceptable; the act of accepting; the fact of being accepted, as in approval. It further adds, acceptance can mean to endure without protest or reaction; to regard as proper, normal, or inevitable; to recognize as true.

When my heart is screaming "NO!" and rejecting every aspect of a situation, what would it mean if I had to accept it? That I approve or agree with what happened? That I'm fine with it?

No, there are some things in life that I would never want in a million years and that I could never be fine with – my son's death for example. I will never like it, approve of it, or endorse it. I will also never get over it, if that means feeling, thinking, and acting exactly like I did before he died. The fact that this huge life transition was forced upon me in a most tragic way means I could not possibly embrace this change. Yet, here I was, in the midst of a profound shift and I couldn't quite figure out how to proceed.

All these years later, I have arrived at a definition more in line with the second dictionary meaning that works for me, and I offer it to you. Acceptance means getting to the point where I acknowledge my reality without shock, denial, or resistance. It is what it is (not in a dismissive way, but in an all-encompassing way). It doesn't mean I'm pleased about the situation or that I don't care. And it certainly doesn't mean I don't continue to have strong feelings about it. Acceptance to me is intimately knowing and understanding my own reality; facing my truth and staring it in the eye. And reality includes both thoughts and emotions.

Moving beyond shock is a normal process that obviously takes time. When my son died, it was a long time before the news was old and a familiar part of me. Even when someone is ill, or you learn other distressing facts, there is still that moment when you realize your world is irrevocably altered. I've found that the same thought that is shocking at one moment seems much less intense once it's old news. I remember yearning for that time to arrive.

Moving beyond resistance requires some resolve. Let's face it: it makes sense to resist pain and tragedy. Who would welcome it? In the beginning, feeling resistant toward heartbreak is entirely reasonable. The difficulty comes if we remain resistant to our circumstances and keep trying to hold onto some version of life as it used to be. Ongoing resistance can lead to enduring denial.

Moving beyond denial can be tricky because a certain amount of denial at the time of a crisis is adaptive and protects us from an overload of pain. Denial becomes problematic when it continues and keeps us from ultimately dealing with our feelings. I remember those first feelings of unreality – that sense of things being surreal. It was impossible to wrap my mind around what had happened. But eventually, the truth of the situation took hold, and that's when I began to feel all my emotions.

Exploring Emotions

This is the time to explore our emotions. I use the word "explore" because there are many ways to work with our inner responses. Exploration requires curiosity, and willingness to try out different approaches to see what's useful in various circumstances. Try not to be afraid of or judge your feelings; take them out, turn them upside down and inside out, look at them from all sides. Share them, take breaks from them, and get to know them as well as you can. Notice as they shift and evolve over time. You are a remarkable and unique individual with an emotional experience all your own. Honor it, and you honor yourself.

Just naming emotions seems to calm the fight-flight-or-freeze response that can keep us on high alert. So what is a feeling? Here's a handy guide. A word is a feeling if the phrase "I feel __" can be replaced with "I am __." For example, "I feel cold" expresses a feeling and I can accurately replace it with "I am cold." Similarly, "I am frustrated, angry, overwhelmed, hurt, lost, discombobulated," etc., all communicate feelings.

If you find yourself thinking or saying, "I feel *that*…," this is an expression of a belief or thought since it wouldn't make sense to say, "I am that…" While beliefs and thoughts are important, see if you can detect the feelings connected to your thoughts.

Once you identify your feelings, try not to judge them. Remember they are not good or bad, they just are. While certain emotions may be more pleasant or unpleasant to experience, the fact that you have a certain feeling is actually a neutral statement and not (for example) a commentary on your worth as an individual.

Having our emotions validated is a powerfully healing experience. Validation refers to telling someone how you feel and having them acknowledge it and hold it without trying to make it go away. Validating statements include anything we can say yes to.

"You're so sad." Yes

"This is such a hard time." Yes.

"You really miss him (or her)." Yes.

Such statements, while seemingly obvious, make us feel heard, seen, understood, and supported. It reminds us that even in the most difficult of circumstances we are not alone, which is comforting.

Validation does not include statements that try to push us into a more positive state.

"At least he didn't suffer."

"He's in a better place."

"You should be over it by now."

"Stop feeling sorry for yourself."

These statements are all dismissive and unfeeling. Can you imagine hearing one of these and replying, "Oh, you're right – I think I'll be happy instead!" Most likely the speaker is uncomfortable with our anguish and can't go there with us, or they desperately want us to feel better and don't know what else to say. Either way, this may be the best they can do at this moment, and we need to find others (including ourselves) for support and validation.

While it's important to give yourself permission to feel your feelings, you also get to choose the moments and duration of your emotional explorations. Some feelings are difficult to tolerate for very long, and some are inconvenient to experience in certain settings. As long as you do not deny what you feel and you don't refuse to feel, you do get to choose when, where, with whom, and for how long you attend to your feelings in any given session.

Especially when feelings are tough and intense, purposeful distraction can provide a useful respite and pave the way to more meaningful exploration later on. Imagine your inner self carefully and lovingly wrapping up those feelings in a beautiful box and setting it gently on a shelf in a corner of your mind. You know where it is, and you know you'll return to re-open the box and work again with its contents. Just don't forget about it completely because forsaken emotions tend to find you and demand urgent attention when you least expect it.

Did you know that under certain circumstances you can choose a feeling? Again, make sure you're not ignoring what's organically there, but there may be some moments when you decide to try on a positive feeling that's different from your natural state during times of challenge. This is sort of like "fake it till you make it," and while I don't advocate using this strategy as a default setting, it can be a nice intermittent reminder of what's possible in the future. As such, it can instill hope when times seem hopeless and provide another type of temporary respite. Periodic recharging and re-energizing can help you navigate continuing grief.

I remember times I felt lost and unsure what to do, how to proceed, or which action to take. In these moments, I learned to shift my focus from *doing* to *being*. That is, I stopped asking what I wanted to do and began to consider instead who I am or may want to become. What are my values and motivations? This has always clarified my thinking.

With a nod to the mindfulness movement and to DBT (Dialectical Behavioral Therapy), "knowing" is complex and consists of both analytical thinking and simply observing one's experience. Society puts so much emphasis on *doing* that little attention is usually paid to *being.* But combining the two, balancing them, and learning to appropriately switch back and forth can actually help us access our wisdom

So how do we step into our *being* mind? By watching, recording, and sensing without judgment. By accepting everything from physical sensations to the experience of our immediate environment. And by acknowledging the unique and special human being, each of us certainly is.

More acceptance. Not only are we being asked to accept a new situation, we also have to accept a new version of ourselves. Accepting oneself doesn't mean we're perfect or finished evolving. It only means we recognize where we're at right now and it's okay. Think of it as radical acceptance that doesn't require any prerequisite. I like to use a line taken from EFT (Emotional Freedom Techniques or "Tapping"): "Even though I'm ....(fill in the blank), I deeply and completely accept myself."

What is Healing?

When I was a kid and fell off my bike, I wasn't surprised to see a scraped knee and feel the sting of wounded flesh (and pride!). It didn't take long for a scab to form, and even though I didn't like that crusty and stiff brown cover, I knew it meant I was healing. Then came the inevitable itching, until finally, the scab fell off to almost magically reveal brand new skin. Depending on the injury, there was sometimes a scar, but one fact remained clear: my body had an amazing ability to heal.

Fast forward an unmentionable number of years, and here I am trying to make sense of other kinds of injuries and our capacity to heal from them. It's true, I'm thinking about much more complex suffering than just a skinned knee. Do our wounded hearts, minds, and spirits also have that healing ability? I absolutely believe they do.

To me, emotional healing involves a course of renewal. It means I am moving forward even though I'm going through a major life upheaval. I will never be the same; I can't go "back to normal" no matter how much I wish I could. In fact, I may always struggle with some aspect of this challenge; I may feel a bit more vulnerable. But this is the new me – bruises and all – trying to greet each new day as it unfolds and be able to function in my new circumstances.

Healing is not the same as a cure. Many of us get hung up on the word cure because it implies "good as new," "as if the problem never happened" or that the suffering can never return. Since we can't predict the future, the idea of healing seems to more appropriately fit real life. It acknowledges what we've been through, our learning to cope with reality, and our sense of gaining some insight about ourselves as we go through life.

Rather than being a one-time event, I believe healing is a process in which we engage whenever we're trying to recover from a painful loss. Since this pain usually involves some type of unwelcome change that requires giving up familiar (and perhaps life-long) thoughts or behavior patterns, the healing process will naturally impact our ongoing relationships and ability to function into the future.

Looking back at all of my unwelcome transitions, I recognize a consistent practice that has benefited me: telling my story. I felt a need to give voice to my experience to help make it real, and since I happen to be comfortable writing, journaling came naturally to me.

I wrote to chronicle what was happening, my observations, and what they meant to me. Sometimes it didn't matter whether or not these entries were read; it was the expression that was important. Sometimes I sent my journal entries to select others. Each time I wrote, I felt somehow unburdened. I also felt a sense of accomplishment at having documented my personal experience. Some people use blogs for this purpose, and I think it's a great way to tell your story.

I also needed to *talk* about my journey. I talked to friends, relatives, and my therapist. As I told my story, I felt validated in just being listened to. Even though there are some losses no one can understand unless they've been through them, I could feel my listeners' care and compassion. This meant the world to me and was part of my healing.

At various times I created scrapbooks, photo albums, and collages that conveyed certain aspects of a given story. I know others who paint, make jewelry, and write music to communicate their experience. There really is no limit to the creative ways we can express ourselves, and they're all good. I find creativity to be satisfying and healing, and I highly recommend it.

Some people start to write, speak, and/or create as soon as they're aware of an unwelcome change they need to accept. Others need time to absorb the shock and find some measure of equilibrium. You'll know when you're ready.

Whatever activities or projects you choose to begin, don't think of Acceptance as a destination at which you'll arrive. Accepting is an ongoing process that changes and evolves with us as we continue to grow.

Chapter Summary

In this chapter, you learned a modified definition of accepting; one more in keeping with the actual experience of losing a loved one. You read about validating all your thoughts and feelings and the benefit of doing so. Finally, you considered what healing is in the context of grief.

What's Ahead

You may be wishing for some examples and stories of accepting. The next chapter takes all this theory and describes what accepting can actually look and feel like.

Stories of Accepting

"For after all, the best thing one can do when it is raining is let it rain."

~ Henry Wadsworth Longfellow

Now that we know what accepting is and isn't (or doesn't have to be), let's discuss specifically what it's like in the Four Facets framework.

In this chapter, I present examples of what accepting can look and feel like. They come from my own experiences and those of others. All were learned by struggling through loss. Your personal path may be different; these stories are meant to inspire your own insights and creative ways of inhabiting your reality.

The Big Wave

Since we know accepting is the opposite of fighting against something, here's an analogy I frequently use.

Imagine yourself at the beach, standing at the water's edge. Waves roll in periodically, and you watch as they become stronger and more forceful. You turn away from the surf, ready to play a little guessing game – how long until the next wave comes? With your back to the water, you have no idea when to prepare. And besides, you get distracted by some gulls flying overhead.

Suddenly, you're pummeled by a surge of water; you're caught off guard, gasping for air and struggling to keep your balance. You vow to be better prepared for the next one, and you are ... slightly.

You tune your hearing into the cadence of the oncoming waves and try to recognize the nearness of each one. You count the seconds between the swells but never come to a reliable interval. So you grind your feet into the sand and brace yourself for the next dousing onslaught.

After a few more soakings, you realize nature is just too unpredictable. You relax your stance a bit, bringing some bounce into your legs. You sharpen your listening still further and begin to detect each wave's approach and take a breath just before it hits. The waves rock you, but you're still standing. Rather than struggling against their power, you let each one wash over you as it dissipates back out to sea.

You become attuned to the rhythm of this advance and retreat, each time, allowing a full drenching. Soon you recognize that your stance is much more stable than before, with your feet firmly rooted in the wet sand. Eventually, the tide recedes and calm returns to the beach.

Sometimes we know when a new wave of grief is likely, and other times, it catches us by surprise. There really is no way to predict them with complete accuracy and somehow prepare. And even though the passing years generally decrease their frequency and intensity, an unexpectedly rough surge can happen at any time. The best we can do is to know they will come and stay calm and flexible.

Easier said than done, I know. In the days after my son died, accepting meant I needed to touch something of his nearly every moment. I carried around a stuffed bear from his childhood. I slept with it, held it on my lap, ate with it next to my plate. It felt necessary to be as connected as possible to a part of him, and it was also proof that he was my little boy. As I yielded to the structure and rhythm of making funeral arrangements, organizing photo collage boards, and letting close friends handle everything else, I was still aware of a protective detachment from my emotions. I was grateful for it, and at the same time, I wondered how long it would last. Things just seemed strangely incongruous: David's name did not belong in an obituary; it was more suitable on a diploma or award certificate.

The day after the funeral, during shiva and with a house full of people, the detachment suddenly lifted. In one moment, I became overwhelmed by the realization that David no longer walked the earth *anywhere.* A dear friend escorted me swiftly upstairs and sat with me until the fits of sobbing subsided. I learned that like the waves on the beach, these outbreaks of anguish had a schedule all their own and that I could only surrender to their power. Although I had no energy to do otherwise, I believe giving in to the flow of tears was actually useful.

There were times I was struck by the unfairness of my loss. When I would see someone on a motorcycle riding without a helmet, I'd wonder, "Why does he get to live and David had to die," remembering the lectures *he gave me* on his commitment to motorcycle safety. It's true – there is absolutely nothing fair about any of this. And yet, it is reality.

I became aware that I was now a member of a group to which no one wants to belong: parents whose children have died. I wasn't ready to join a support group, but I did email The Compassionate Friends who sent me a packet for the newly bereaved. It was very strange to think back over the years when I provided grief support to parents who were going through what I was now experiencing.

Time

As the days after David's death became weeks, I kept track of how long it had been since he was last alive. "This time last week he was still with us." "Three weeks ago today, we were talking about his trip to England." Knowing I'd always remember the summer of 2011 as the season of David's death, and therefore, the last time he was alive, I didn't want summer to end. Being in that time frame felt like an important connection to him. But as the leaves started to turn colors and the air began to chill that fall, it seemed I was being pushed further away from my son. The approach of autumn felt wrong, like a betrayal and abandonment of him. No matter how much I longed to remain in his last season on earth, I could not. I literally felt like I was being forcibly pushed along by time.

Time never asked if I was ready; it just continued its relentless march and pushed me along with it. Soon it was David's birthday (he would have been 27 then) and Halloween, then Thanksgiving and the holiday season. Each special day brought a new wave of grief that I couldn't wait to get past.

New Year's arrived. Leaving the last year of David's life was the most difficult of all. There was no turning back; no, wait, one more minute. The ball dropped, the page turned, and I was in a different year.

Later on, ideas about time came up in a different context. One year I was thinking about my son's then upcoming 31st birthday and my plan to mark the actual day by attending a mindfulness meditation and yoga retreat. Later that week, our family would present the annual David Field Memorial Leadership Award at the company where he worked and had been so successful. It was then just over 4 years since his death. It's always hard to believe I haven't seen him in so long and feel how much I miss him. At the same time, I'm aware that I'm getting used to his not being here.

I mused about what life was like before he was even born, and it struck me that I lived without him then, too. How different it was then! And how fascinating that there was no missing him before his lifetime began, but acute longing afterward.

"Before" and "after" – constructs that are uniquely related to human experience, but do they exist independently in the universe? Einstein believed that time was really an illusion and was relative only to the perspective of the observer. Others have written that time is merely something humans use to measure days and organize our activities or commitments.

As scientists continue to debate the true nature of time, it's certainly not up to me to figure it out. The discussion, however, allows me to consider a few "what-ifs."

- What if time really were an illusion?
- What if "before" and "after" don't really exist?
- What if loss was related to time?
- What if I could feel like I did before David was born?
- What if I could simultaneously hold that feeling while remembering, loving, and appreciating him?
- What if I could accumulate present moments without organizing them into a timeline?

Before you think I've totally lost my mind, let me reassure you that I'm well grounded in reality. It's just that brainstorming possibilities (even outrageous ones) is also a favorite pastime and helps the ongoing work of accepting. In my experience, any shift in perspective can be potentially healing. Each of us gets to try on and play around with ideas, assess their fit, and keep or discard accordingly.

I know I'm not alone in experiencing time as sometimes going too fast and sometimes too slow. And it's not only a function of grief; most of us tend to live either too much in the past or the future, and we end up not really noticing the present. Unchecked, we could end up wishing or worrying our lives away.

Mindfulness – Accepting Thoughts and Feelings

A few years ago, I decided to try practicing mindfulness in a more, well, mindful way. This means I've been trying to pay attention to what is, without judgment. Anything in life can be done mindfully: eating, working, playing, resting. Tuning into one's present experience and returning to that awareness when the mind wanders (as it always does) keeps us anchored in the moment. Mindfulness is thought to be helpful for coping with many of life's difficulties. I find it fosters appreciation, gratitude, and patience, all of which I need more of while grieving.

Some thoughts from those early attempts at mindfulness:

"Right now, I'm sitting at my desk writing on my laptop. I'm sipping a cup of tea as I write and occasionally gaze out the window. It's snowing again. A million thoughts try to compete for my attention: cleaning my car later, my to-do list, memories, worries. I take another sip of tea and gently bring myself back to writing. I am writing. Writing and sipping. They're two simple acts that ground me in the present where memories don't haunt, and worries don't matter. I feel peaceful and grateful."

Sometimes, accepting and being mindful means allowing yourself to feel difficult feelings. Grief is always with you even when you're not directly feeling it. As a grieving parent said, "You never know when it's going to poke its head out and say, 'Hey, look at me, I'm back to visit for a bit!"

While in most cases, it's typical to try to push the pain away; to end it as quickly as possible, there are those moments when you are just enveloped in agony. Going into the suffering for a while helps anchor it in the mind and heart, which truly allows you to inhabit your reality. Friends and family may not understand this, as they can't bear to see you and experience you in pain.

Then there is the topic of impermanence. I struggled mightily when I first started thinking deeply about impermanence. I wanted to have things (including relationships) in my life organized so that I could count on them. When I had to accept the reality that nothing is permanent, I actually felt angry and betrayed. Through the years, I've learned that change is part of living. Sometimes impermanence is hard to tolerate, and sometimes we depend on it.

Certain days, like birthdays and death anniversaries, are going to be extra difficult and that's to be expected. Sometimes the anticipation of those days is actually worse than the day itself. One mother pointed out the possibility that in a drawn-out dying process (prolonged illness or life support), you may start feeling down around the time of the event that started them toward death. She advises not to berate yourself for feeling sad; acknowledge and accept it. It's certainly okay to be sad, to hurt, to cry, to be angry, and to be a little more short tempered. This too shall pass.

Our culture tells us, "Don't cry," even when crying is the most natural thing in the world. There is a stigma about grieving; it evokes anxiety and misunderstanding. People around us want it to end. The truth is that grief never ends because the pain of losing someone doesn't just go away. It's a constant companion with whom we must forge an unwelcome friendship. So there is no arrival point at which we're "done" and "back to normal." Life without our loved ones is the new normal, and it's up to each of us to figure out how to navigate it. An essential aspect of this is acknowledging our story and our feelings.

Especially difficult is the seeming erasure of our loved one's existence. Taking names off doors, deleting cell phone numbers, taking down Facebook pages, even throwing out any scraps of paper with their handwriting on it can be impossible to consider. These are, perhaps, the last physical bonds we have with them, and they are comforting. Even though they also bring pangs of sadness, the sad feeling becomes a familiar companion and is ultimately more comfortable than the pain of nonexistence.

One bereaved mother wrote, "Don't worry that you still have not been able to clean their room out even years after. Some people will do that right away and others, maybe, never. It doesn't mean that you're not accepting their death if you find you wish to keep their room intact. Sometimes, that room is a safe haven where you can go and just 'be' with them."

We each get to grieve in our own way in our own time. There are no rules, so choose what seems okay for now. We, humans, are constantly evolving and so is our grief.

Chapter Summary

In this chapter, you read about the Big Wave analogy and learned about my personal experience of accepting my son's death. You considered various insights about time and its illusory qualities, and how mindfulness has helped me accept the painful thoughts and feelings of grief.

What's Ahead

In the next chapter, you'll find a list of ideas to build your **Accepting** skills. These are steps you can take right now, so turn the page to get started!

Accepting Skill-Building Tips

"Facing it, always facing it, that's the way to get through. Face it."

~ Joseph Conrad

Incorporating insights from the two previous chapters on accepting, this chapter offers practical skill-building ideas for you to consider. There is no order in which to try them; they are randomly numbered.

Each tip is meant to encourage you on your grief journey and to inspire further exploration into what works specifically for you. Please feel free to ignore anything that doesn't resonate, or that feels "icky." Please also modify items in ways that stir your creativity and add these ideas to your list for future reference.

1. Start a journal of your thoughts and feelings, acknowledging what you can't change.
2. Learn as much as you can about the situation to understand the facts, but pay attention to how much information you can comfortably consume.
3. Start a grief blog.
4. Describe your sensations and feelings, not what you think about them or how you want them to change. Don't judge them.
5. Accept your sensations and feelings. Notice them and be willing to have them even if they're uncomfortable.
6. Write the story of what happened.
7. Publish a book about what happened and your grief journey.
8. Write poems about your experience.
9. Record your story on your phone's app.
10. Talk to a friend who can listen, doesn't need to fix, and doesn't have an agenda for you.
11. Talk to a therapist or counselor with whom you feel a connection.
12. Talk to a clergy person with whom you feel a connection.
13. Join a support group.
14. Write a letter to your loved one.
15. Make a scrapbook.
16. Create a photo memory collage.
17. Create a photo memory book.
18. Create a memory quilt or have one made.

19. Write a song to or about your loved one.

20. Learn to meditate.

21. Learn and practice mindfulness exercises. (Breathing; progressive relaxation; etc.) Don't get caught up in constant busy-ness.

22. Meditate on impermanence/change.

23. Ask for tolerance and help in accepting from whatever force you believe in. It could be the Universe, your sense of the Divine, Mother Nature, or any power greater than you.

24. Draw or paint your memories and feelings.

25. Make or wear original jewelry pieces in honor of your loved one.

26. Find appropriate distractions that work for you and use them to take breaks from distress. Alternating between facing the pain and distraction from it helps ease the process of accepting.

Chapter Summary

In this chapter, you reviewed a list of tips that can build your accepting skills. You identified which might be realistic for you and which hints need further thought. You might have even thought of your own ideas for moving forward through accepting.

What's Ahead

You're about to start Part Two: Adapting. In the next chapter, you will learn why adapting to your new reality is important and how to begin to embrace it

PART TWO

Adapting

Adapting to a New Reality

> "When we are no longer able to change a situation, we are challenged to change ourselves."
>
> ~ Viktor Frankl

Now we turn to the inevitable question: How will I go on? In this chapter, I discuss the definition of adapting and offer various ways of coping with a new reality, even when it's a heartbreaking one. From my own perspective and that of others, I consider the human craving for order, using appropriate distraction, and ponder the question, "Who am I now?" I also offer insights about getting through holidays when you're grieving.

~

As much as I didn't want to believe my son was dead, I eventually had to acknowledge this reality. And in addition to the pain of losing him, I struggled mightily with the question, "How am I going to go on?" This dilemma stops us in our tracks and is the most persistent and universal concern I hear in my practice and have confronted in my life.

Google defines adapting as making something suitable for a new use or purpose; modifying. It can also mean becoming adjusted to new conditions. That's just fine when the new purpose or conditions are happy or even neutral ones. But adapting to unwelcome change can seem impossible, especially when it takes a long time just to wrap your mind and heart around what has happened.

After a major life transition like losing a loved one, every aspect of life is going to be different. Even though you may find yourself longing for how things used to be and the way you used to do things, the truth is that you now must navigate life in a new way. This is both difficult and necessary.

When I first heard my son was killed, an anguished "NO!" rose up from my heart and screamed into the night. There was no accepting, no understanding, and certainly no will to adapt. But over time, I recognized that change was here whether I liked it or not. I had to stop staring at a closed door and find a way to turn the no into a yes. Not yes in the sense that it's okay or that I like it. But yes meaning I will inhabit my reality and move forward through it.

Keep Learning

Our brains crave information and order. It's natural to long for as much detail as possible about your particular situation, its effects, and how you're coping. What specifics do you know about what happened? Who might be responsible? How will you go on? Could it have been avoided or prevented? If so, how?

These are hard questions to ponder, and they come up whether we want them to or not. Just know this is part of the grief process. We typically begin to draw conclusions based on limited information. After all, any answer feels better than no answer, even if we have to guess or make something up. If something seems out of order, we tend to mull it over in our minds until it makes sense.

What conclusions have you reached that result from your craving for order? What information do you still need to make sense of your situation? It's typical to alternate between focusing on the details of the loss and pondering how to go on. But make no mistake: going on means creating a new order out of chaos and sorrow. Anything that brings even a minute sense of tidiness to your life will help you with adapting.

Part of the process includes coping with sometimes surprising feelings. Many people struggle with anger, guilt, or anxiety after a loved one has died, and these may be confusing to navigate. Try to remember there are no wrong emotions; they are proof of how difficult it is to adapt to this new reality. Are any of your feelings based on assumptions you've made that may or may not be accurate? Sometimes it's neater to believe things would have been different "if only..." than to sit with the ambiguity of "maybe."

Research how other people cope with similar circumstances. Identify an appropriate use of distraction without going into denial. Read books; visit online resources; access support organizations. Learn something new ... it jump-starts your thinking and creativity which, in turn, increases your sense of stability.

Identity

Death forces us to re-examine who we are. If you have lost a child (or children), are you still a parent? When someone asks how many children you have, what do you say? If your husband died, are you still a wife? When my sister died, did that mean I was no longer a sibling?

Adapting to our dear one's death means figuring out who we are now, without them. But it's not as if they never lived, so this pursuit takes time and patience. We have to re-define our family roles and how we relate to others in our environment. We also need to discover our strengths, limitations, and ways of functioning through new eyes and with a new perspective.

Take a Grief Break

Sometimes facing the anguish of loss can make you feel like you're losing your mind. It can be hard to concentrate or do everyday tasks, and you may feel heartbroken.

It's okay to have a respite from misery.

I am not advocating living in denial. It is important to acknowledge reality and to face feelings. What I know from experience is that taking occasional breaks from unrelenting pain can actually help us tolerate it better over time.

Dialectical Behavior Therapy (DBT) offers several strategies for distracting ourselves from distress, using the acronym DISTRACT. I have adapted these skills for those who are grieving. Try as many as you can, and note which ones work for you (these are very individual so remember there is no right or wrong). Regular practice will make your favorites become second nature and available whenever you need them.

- **D**o something else, to feel something different. Watch a movie, go for a walk, play a game or sport, garden go shopping, do a hobby. Volunteer your time at an organization meaningful to you, help a friend with a project or childcare, do something nice for someone. Do anything you enjoy that you can really get involved in.

- **I**mages of something different can create different feelings. Imagine something else that doesn't remind you of your pain. Bring comforting and soothing images to mind. What you think about, remember, and imagine causes you to feel it in the moment, so focus on something that makes you feel good. Think about what can go right and is pleasant. Remember that what fills our minds fuels our emotions.

- **S**ensations can distract you from your current pain. Use your five senses: seeing, hearing, tasting, touching, and smelling. Some people add laughing and loving. Look for and create situations in which you can engage your senses to feel differently. For example, look at the most beautiful painting or photo you can find, listen to your favorite uplifting music, taste delicious flavors, use an ice pack to feel intense cold or take a hot bath, and inhale the fragrance of your favorite perfume or cookies baking in the oven.

- **T**hink of something else that creates other feelings. You can do this through reading, watching videos, or just thinking about something that takes you away from your loss. Try something funny, fascinating or creatively engrossing like crossword puzzles, Words with Friends, or writing a poem.

- **R**emember other memories than those that cause your current pain. Call up your favorite happy memories and revel in the joy they bring. I found it comforting to remember pleasant times before my son was born. It reminded me that I am capable of joy even without his physical presence.

- **Ac**cept that pain is a part of life; you can take it. None of us gets through life without loss. I wondered how other people have coped with losing their children, and I began researching their stories. I realized I'm a member of a large club no one wants to join, and that belonging to this group is neither exclusive nor special. It can happen to anyone, anywhere, and somehow we all find ways of going on.

- **T**ake an alternative approach; behave differently than how your feelings tell you to behave. Even though you feel like lying on the couch, take your dog for a walk. Even though you want to isolate and stay home, meet a friend for lunch or book a spa day. Many typical activities seem daunting through the agony of loss; allowing yourself a little of these can be healing

Distracting yourself from the discomfort of grief is meant to be a temporary respite. Use the strategies that work for you, always returning to the undeniable reality of what is. And ask for help when you need it.

Holidays

As anyone who has ever been through heartbreak will agree, holiday time presents a special challenge. With images of joy, fun, and happy families everywhere, it can feel incompatible with any kind of traumatic loss. Some want to skip the holidays altogether, sensing that the pain of loss is just too raw and instead of being ready to celebrate you may feel more like hiding.

For me, the sadness of my son's death makes it challenging at times to feel celebratory. I will always miss him, and his absence is sometimes like a heavy weight across my shoulders. There were years I felt like an observer at holiday gatherings; sort of there in body but not a true participant. Other seasons, I've noticed a readiness to be with family and friends, and yet the healing process still includes moments of weariness.

TV commercials and sitcoms show us incredibly happy people enjoying their holidays; workplaces and homes are decorated, and music reminds us to be of good cheer. The inherent expectations of happiness, merriment, and celebration can seem, frankly, impossible. My realization that life had irrevocably changed forced me to invent new ways of moving through each day in order to shape this new reality. If every aspect of life was going to be different, I could actually choose how I wanted to observe special days.

Despite those TV ads, not everyone is happily enjoying the holiday season every minute. There are mixed feelings for most people, relating to losses, memories, worries, and realizations. These mixed feelings mean we can hold seemingly opposing emotions at the same time. For example, there's a part of me that is so sad my son can't be at our holiday table, and there's another part of me that delights in the joy of my grandchildren. We can grieve our losses at the same time we're grateful for our blessings. They coexist without canceling one another out.

The most important thing I've learned about holidays is to plan ahead. Don't wait until the day arrives to think about how you want to spend it. Take some time imagining different options (this is where you can get creative), as adapting cherished traditions or creating new ones can be very meaningful. Discuss your thoughts with family members and enlist their support. Remember, you don't have to decide how to spend every holiday from now on; you're just figuring out how to observe this day this year.

Our culture puts a lot of emphasis on celebrating the holidays. You may not be ready to make a decision about how to spend a particular day, and pressure to do so may increase your stress. Give yourself a break – it's okay to modify, postpone, or otherwise revise former traditions. Try something different and then see how it feels; you'll adjust future plans from there. Remember it's *a* day; not *the* day.

Have realistic expectations at this time of year. As you decide on your holiday schedule, keep an eye on your energy level to avoid being overwhelmed. Are you really up for having the whole gang over and doing all the cooking this year? Do you feel like attending office parties and other get-togethers? How might you modify your usual holiday routine? Decide what is doable for you and stick to it. It's okay to say no to one-too-many invitations.

Identify a support person who will check in with you periodically throughout the day or evening. When you're going through a difficult time, you might not recognize a need to take a break, go for a walk, or even go and lie down for a little while. Tell them you need to hear your loved one's name. Your support person and you can develop a signal that communicates, "Get me out of here," if you do become exhausted or stressed.

When life hurts, it's hard to get out of your own pain. Sometimes the best way to cope and soothe the discomfort of loss during the holidays is to help others. Volunteer some time to any organization that benefits those in need, as long as it fits with your values and feels healing. Some people serve meals to the homeless; others bring toys to hospital pediatric playrooms. I even heard of someone who brought dinner to a police station on Christmas Eve. Make sure your volunteer work is realistic for you at that time. If you're hosting a holiday meal (and you have plenty of help), you can also invite someone who doesn't have a place to go this year. You can probably think of many other possibilities. The important thing is to make a positive difference to someone else, which helps you feel warm inside.

It's important to know and honor your Self as you go through the holiday season. Choose ways of adapting and coping that make sense for you. Pay attention to sleep, nutrition, exercise, solitude, and togetherness. Honor your own spirituality. My touchstone is always to ask myself if something feels healing, and I offer that if it's useful for you. You will also come up with your own criteria for determining holiday options.

Chapter Summary

In Chapter 5, you learned what adapting means in the context of grief and that it is normal to crave information and order following the death of someone you love. You also explored the appropriate use of distraction and how loss impacts our sense of identity. Finally, you considered the challenge of getting through holidays during this difficult time.

What's Ahead

In the next chapter, Stories of Adapting, you will read how I and others have navigated death anniversaries and various holidays. There are also stories about the dual nature of memory and how forgiveness can heal. For a peek inside personal experience, turn the page.

Stories of Adapting

"Intelligence is the ability to adapt to change."

~ Stephen Hawking

This chapter presents personal accounts of adapting to loss. Here are stories about navigating death anniversaries and various holidays. I describe the different roles memory can play and how forgiveness has moved me forward in adjusting to a new normal. Finally, I discuss the difference between reacting and responding, and how each may be utilized in grief.

~

Death Anniversaries

There are certain dates we'll just never forget. Dates when everything changed; that mark a new reality; that seem to require some type of observance. 9/11 is one such date, forever seared in our American consciousness as the moment this generation lost its national innocence along with so many precious souls.

Anytime we sustain a life-altering loss, we tend to note the passage of time since that day and calendar our journey in its wake.

Each year, as I approach the anniversary of my son's death on July 24th, I think about what happened that day and how much I miss him, and also about what I've learned since then. I quickly discovered that arriving at the date without a plan was extra difficult. I learned to think ahead about how I might want to observe the day.

With each year finding me in a somewhat different emotional place, I found myself choosing various options over time. Sometimes I felt better working (and thereby focusing on and helping others), and some years I was grateful the date fell on a weekend so I could plan something else meaningful. There were days I've wanted to be alone, just reflecting on my thoughts and feelings, and other times, I've gone for long walks at the Botanic Garden with another bereaved mother.

My faith tradition – Judaism – provides me with a built-in way of marking this anniversary. The Yiddish word "Yahrzeit" literally translates to "time of year" and is noted by lighting a Yahrzeit candle at home and attending services in which your loved one's name is said aloud. Although undeniably sad, this ritual puts me in touch with the support of my community, both those who just happened to come to services that night and other mourners as well. It normalizes the experience of grief within the context of ongoing life.

Mother's Day

No matter what your current situation might be, Mother's Day evokes strong feelings about our families. As a bereaved mother, this national celebration of motherhood is challenging. I miss my son more than words can describe, and I wish he were here.

Each year, I take out the Mother's Day cards he had given me in the last few years of his life (the "adult" cards – the ones where he wrote funny or beautiful notes to me before signing). I arrange them carefully along with my current cherished cards from my daughter and grandsons.

If David's absence were the only thing I focused on, Mother's Day would be nearly unbearable. But I'm so grateful to have my wonderful daughter, stepdaughters, grandsons, and granddaughters right here with me now!

They continue to be the light of my life, and I feel true joy in their love and presence.

Is it possible to feel both the sadness of loss and the joy of gratitude at the same exact time? Yes, absolutely.

I will always miss David; that's just not going to change. My daughter misses her brother profoundly, and my grandsons miss their fun-loving uncle. Having loved ones who share this loss helps me feel less alone in my grief, and remembering him with them seems to solidify his ongoing presence in our lives.

At the same time, I want to ensure that David's death has not overshadowed my life; that I'm not so focused on who's not here that I can't enjoy who is. I have arrived at a place in which I'm grieving my loss and celebrating my treasures at the same time. It feels right.

I know others who are experiencing their first Mother's Day without their mother. Even though someone may have lived a long life, it's hard to face a national tribute to the person who has always been there, but is no longer. I'm sure they are also feeling sadness and joy at the same time – sorrow for her absence and joy that she lived a long, remarkable life as their mother.

I also know a young woman delighting in her first Mother's Day as a mom. Mixed in with all the happiness of new life might be some sorrow in missing previous generations of family who would have adored this eagerly awaited gift.

There are so many variations on the theme of concurrent joy and sorrow; as humans, we all have this capacity, and I'm sure you have your own stories. Find a supportive person or group and tell them; grab your journal and write them. It's evidence of our humanity.

Halloween

I see the signs everywhere: neighboring homes draped in faux spider webbing; bright orange pumpkins waiting to be transformed into Jack-O-Lanterns; costumes and candy overflowing store shelves. I know Halloween is approaching, and it seems everyone is eagerly anticipating the fun.

Everyone, except for me.

I never used to be such a humbug about this holiday. I have many fond memories of my own childhood candy-begging, and I really enjoyed accompanying my children and grandchildren (looking exceptionally adorable) on their yearly rounds. But things are different now.

I noticed my changed outlook for the first time just 3 months after David's death. The witches and goblins, and really, anything humorously portrayed, didn't bother me so much. What shook me was seeing suburban lawns decorated like cemeteries, some with plastic body parts poking up from the pretend graves.

I instantly flashed back to David's broken body nestled in its casket; my tearful kisses bidding him goodbye for the last time. I thought about the dozens of red roses we tossed into his grave, and the care with which we later chose his memorial marker ... to honor the wonderful young man he was and to ensure his eternal memory.

At the second Halloween after David's passing, I recognized I wasn't quite as distressed as the previous year. As I thought about the meaning of Halloween to me and to our culture in general, I found myself wondering about our collective fascination with the "undead."

Perhaps this is our way of looking our own mortality in the face and making it more tolerable. Maybe joking around about some kind of space between life and death helps us cope with the inevitability of our eventual demise as we confront our greatest fear.

Whatever meaning Halloween conjures up for any individual, I know no one intends for it to be anything but fun. Even the lawns decked out as spooky graveyards aren't meant to hurt anyone or to be insensitive to those who are mourning recently lost loved ones.

This is the nature of loss: there are times when your particular loss overshadows (even temporarily) what used to be ordinary life. It doesn't matter what kind of loss you experience, these moments continue to pop up, sometimes when you least expect them.

The couple struggling with infertility who can't stand to see baby product commercials; the recently-divorced woman who just can't share in the excitement of her sister's upcoming wedding; the mother of a child with a severe developmental disability who has trouble listening to other parents complain about typical extra-curricular carpool duties. These are a few examples of loss-related challenges that can affect how we experience life.

Have you noticed yourself or someone else struggling with an aspect of everyday life because of personal loss? If so, you're in good company, for this is one common way we humans tend to cope with unwelcome transitions. The struggle will evolve, it may fade, and it may disappear. And it's all part of the journey.

Memory: Gift or Curse?

Is the memory of a loved one who has died a blessing or a curse?

It can actually be both, depending on the context and situation. Memories can even be a blessing and a curse at the same time.

Supportive Memories

I find it wonderfully supportive when someone mentions my son David's name and remembers him in our lives. You can be sure I'm thinking about him anyway, so it's not possible that you're reminding me of something I've temporarily forgotten.

There is nothing sadder to me than acting as if David never lived. He did live, passionately and fully, even if it was only for 26 years. In that time he had a profoundly positive effect on a lot of people. Because they are all I have left of him, these memories are cherished gifts.

Difficult Memories

I remember, as well, the searing pain of memories shortly after David's death. Back then, the whole idea of his nonexistence was so wrong and unreal that everything in the memory category felt like a kick in the gut.

Choosing and assembling pictures for the funeral photo collages were impossibly painful tasks, and they were ultimately completed by a dear friend. Every remembered argument or misunderstanding brought waves of guilt as I agonized over what wasn't said or how I might have done things differently. Mental reruns of his accident and death plagued my waking hours and disturbed my sleep. These musings did indeed feel like a curse.

Finding My Way

Through my bereavement journey, I've learned to identify what feels healing to me. I realize this is a very personal quest, and each of us needs to assess such things individually.

For me, the belief that David and I can somehow continue our relationship is very healing. So I encourage myself to imagine his loving presence, his influence, his complete awareness, and understanding.

When someone talks to me about him, it enables me to keep him alive in my heart and mind, and he really does continue to "be." I remember the song "My Heart Will Go On" from the Titanic movie. So hauntingly sung by Celine Dion, it captured the certainty that love does indeed continue despite the distance of time and space.

My Message to Family and Friends

I know that some might worry I'll start crying if they talk about David. Well, what's wrong with that? I'd like to declare crying a perfectly acceptable expression of emotion and nothing to fear or worry about!

If I cry, I promise I won't cry forever (even though I felt that way for a long time, too). And if you end up crying with me, then we're sharing something powerful and connecting. That kind of heart-intimacy can be very healing for all of us.

On the other hand, I don't necessarily cry at predictable or anticipated times, and tears can well up when I least expect them and without any obvious trigger. All of this is okay and typical of the grief process, and I don't want you to protect me from any of it.

Bring the Past into the Future

Each time the ball drops, I am carried further away from my last living contact with my son. As the most painful thoughts begin to lose their power, it is the gift of memory that allows him to enter each new year along with me, and I am so grateful for his company.

Words from a bereaved daughter and mother:

"Moving forward does not mean moving away from the person you lost. They will always be with you. There may come a time when you don't constantly think about them. I know with my dad, I loved him dearly, but no, I don't think about him daily and when I do think about him, there is no pain, only love. With my boys, I still think about them every day; I still get sad moments that show up and my eyes well up. But they don't consume me. Grief will eventually become less and less consuming."

The words of a grieving wife:

"When my husband passed away we had been married 32 years. Our lives were so intertwined; most of our day was spent together largely because we worked from home together. The silence in the house reminds me every day how much of his energy had filled this home. To not dwell on the silence and vacancy I keep myself as busy as a hamster on a treadmill."

The words of a bereaved mother:

"You learn, I think especially when you lose a child, who your true friends really are, and who just cannot deal with your loss. You will be surprised. Many bereaved parents have shared that their address book changed quite a bit after the loss of their child. I am still confronted by this, and my feelings for certain friends have changed because they have not been there when I needed them. Some people disappear from your life and there will be new people, some who you might have least expected, who come into your life."

Forgiveness

I'll admit, I've made some awful mistakes in my life. I've said things that shouldn't have been expressed (or perhaps expressed differently), and I've remained quiet when I should have spoken up. I've pulled away from people I really felt close to, and I've allowed frustration to persist for far too long.

I'm not proud of these faults, and I feel bad about the hurt I've caused others ... even inadvertently.

After a lot of reflection, I believe my mistakes usually happen after I've somehow been hurt myself. Either my ego needs were not being met, or I didn't believe myself worthy or capable of anything else in that moment. It's about relationships and expectations and being able to communicate how I really feel.

In my opinion, forgiveness doesn't mean what happened was okay. It means I'm ready to move on from feeling terrible about it.

As in many families, there was unfinished business between us when my son David died so suddenly. At his funeral, the Rabbi led us in what I call a forgiveness exercise that I found powerful, and I offer it here:

In our minds, we asked David to forgive us for anything that was misunderstood, unsaid, undone, or incomplete. And we imagined him bestowing total forgiveness without hesitation and with great love.

Then we imagined David asking our forgiveness for anything that was misunderstood, unsaid, undone, or incomplete. With full hearts and no hesitation, we envisioned ourselves completely forgiving him as well.

This exercise isn't only for the circumstances of death but is also equally effective in any situation where communication (for any reason) isn't possible or likely.

There is one last person I haven't yet discussed forgiving. Myself. Yourself. Ourselves. We are the most difficult persons to forgive because we're generally the hardest on ourselves.

This is the most important time to remember it doesn't mean the mistake was okay (even if it was understandable). You're acknowledging you're ready to move on from all the suffering attached to it. Releasing that suffering brings serenity, peace, and a feeling of lightness that energizes your being.

Reacting vs. Responding

Being human means sometimes we react to people and events, and sometimes we respond to them. What's the difference? A reaction is not calculated; it just happens sort of on its own like when the doctor taps your knee and your foot jerks.

A response is a thoughtful process. You consider how you'd like to respond to a certain situation and figure out reasonable things to say and do.

Strong emotions are clues to our reactions, especially anger or hurt. Take some time to pause, notice what you're feeling, and reflect on their possible causes. Then decide how you want to proceed.

Chapter Summary

You have considered the special challenges of death anniversaries and holidays from a more personal perspective. You've also pondered the different roles memory may play and the healing nature of forgiveness. Lastly, you learned the distinction between reacting and responding and how each impacts adapting to loss.

You may have noticed ways in which your own experience is similar to or different from those described here. That's okay. Keep observing and noting your adapting process.

What's Ahead

What do you do with the insights you've gained from the discussion on adapting? In Chapter 7, you will find a list of action items that you can use to build your personal coping skills. Read on to make this section even more relevant to you.

Adapting Skill-Building Tips

> "Adapt or perish, now as ever, is Nature's inexorable imperative."
>
> ~ H.G. Wells

Are you ready to get busy adapting? This chapter offers practical skill-building ideas for you to contemplate. As in all such chapters, there is no order in which to try them; they are randomly numbered.

Each tip is meant to encourage you on your grief journey and to inspire further exploration into what works specifically for you. Please feel free to ignore anything that doesn't resonate, or that feels "icky." Please also tweak items in ways that stir your creativity.

~

One of the great challenges of grieving is to adjust to a new and unwelcome reality. We have to orient ourselves to our particular environment so well that we learn to navigate within it, and it eventually feels like home. Even if it's not the home we previously envisioned or wanted.

Here are some action steps to consider when adapting to loss.

Getting through the holidays:

How do you get through this time of year when a big part of you doesn't feel like celebrating? It makes sense to feel disconnected from joy during times of loss; it can feel bizarre to have our sadness juxtaposed with the expectation of enjoyment and laughter. Depending on what's going on in your life, you might feel left out, alone, and unable to join in the revelry, like having an invisible disability that no one truly understands.

1. Alternate focusing on your loss and thinking about moving forward. This is part of the healing process. Pay equal and alternating attention to the loss itself and how you're moving through it.
2. Decide what's doable for you this year, and stick to it. Figure out how you can realistically participate in any holiday plan, remembering there's always next year. You don't have to say

yes to everything. Create a blueprint, communicate it, and follow it as best you can.

3. Identify a support person to attend functions with. A spouse/partner, family member, or close friend beside you can help you relax. You can choose a different person for each event or have the same companion throughout the season. Either way, an understanding confidante is always near.

4. Spend time with people you love and feel connected to. Your family's cozy Thanksgiving dinner may feel okay but the big office holiday party may not. Honor your feelings, knowing that this is the time to surround yourself with love.

5. Find a personal meaning for each holiday or event you attend. Maybe it's a spiritual meaning, or perhaps it's a connection to someone important. Choosing a special significance can boost your satisfaction.

6. Keep a gratitude list; include your own accomplishments and gifts. There's no doubt about it, expressing gratitude makes us feel better. Start or end your day noting at least one thing you're grateful for.

7. Recognize when "faking it" is useful and when it's not. Look in the mirror and smile, even if you don't feel happy. See if you can sustain the smile for 2 minutes. Feel better? You get to decide if

acting sociably can help you through a holiday gathering.

8. Exercise regularly. Move your body to stay energized. Find activities you like or that you can motivate yourself to do consistently. Research shows exercise also lifts mood.

9. Get plenty of rest. Challenging circumstances can drain our energy. Try to establish a healthy sleep cycle and allow for downtime.

10. Help someone else. One of the best ways to get out of your own misery is to serve others. This is the perfect time of year to make a positive difference in someone else's life, so find an activity that fits your holiday plan.

11. Learn something new. This jump-starts your thinking and your creativity. Take a class or ask a friend to teach you something, or research a project or idea. Just make sure it's interesting and fun.

12. Watch your alcohol intake ... it's a depressant. Although alcohol does loosen inhibitions, it does not elevate mood. In fact, alcohol's effects can be like taking a depressant, and who want to do that?

13. Get organized. Take some time to map out how you'd like to observe your holidays. Decide which tips you're going to implement and list them in order of importance.

14. Create a list of events and associated tasks (baking, shopping, etc.) remembering to keep it doable and meaningful

15. Schedule all tasks in your calendar so that you're not overwhelmed at the last minute.

16. Don't burden yourself with New Year's resolutions. Take stock of the past year without judgment, ponder your ongoing development and priorities, and then determine the next steps.

17. Create intentions by considering these questions: what would I like to learn this year? What strengths would I like to enhance? What joys can I bring into my life that aren't there now? How might I embody my values and priorities?

Observing Death Anniversaries:

1. Plan ahead for anniversary dates. Think about how you might observe the day and note the possibilities. Keep in mind you may be emotional and remember to be gentle with yourself.

2. Consider how you want to spend the day. If work is optional, figure out if taking the day off or working feels better for you.

3. Spend some quiet time reflecting on this day and your feelings. You might journal or meditate, noticing whatever comes up for you. Acknowledge your own spiritual traditions and preferences.

THE 4 FACETS OF GRIEF

4. Create a ritual that honors your loss – visit the cemetery or memorial place, participate in a healing activity (walk, get a massage), light a candle. This may evolve over time, or you may find something you'd like to repeat each year.

5. Connect with others, either in person or virtually, who can reminisce and acknowledge your transition with you.

6. Honor your memories. You might celebrate your loved one's life with a special meal or gathering.

7. Gather photos, assemble a special album or scrapbook, or make a picture or video collage. Anything creative can feel healing on this day.

8. Volunteer at, or make a donation to, an organization that is meaningful to you.

9. Take a break. If you feel overwhelmed and need a distraction, think ahead about what might be appropriate (see a movie; lunch or dinner with friends).

10. Get plenty of rest. Navigating anniversary dates uses a lot of energy, so take a nap if you need one.

Embracing a fresh start:

I have always been inspired by my son David's ability to embrace each new day. Even as a youngster in the grip of relentless and debilitating depression, he viewed tomorrow as a brand new possibility. I remember thinking, "If David can keep going, so can I." Here is what he taught me.

1. Recognize the value of a clean slate. I believe we all function best when we're open to possibility. Trying to push through the emotional and thought baggage of previous hurts and failures usually leaves us overwhelmed and depleted. A fresh start provides a new energy and motivation.
2. Think small. It doesn't have to be a Clean Slate of Life; it can be a brand new season, month, day, or even hour. In fact, the smaller your scope, the more possibilities there are for renewal.
3. Pause to reflect. Take some time to consider what you've been working toward and how you had planned to get there. Do the goals still make sense? Is your action plan still doable? Have you run into unexpected roadblocks?
4. Keep learning. Are there things you've learned that shed new light on your journey? Whenever I have a disappointing, frustrating, or otherwise negative experience, I ask myself what I can learn from it.
5. Revise if needed. Tweaking, adjusting, modifying; these are all aspects of healthy adaptation and not evidence of failure. We humans wouldn't be here if we didn't have the ability to adapt to changing conditions and insights.

6. Turn the page. Whether it's a new day or a fresh week, embrace the openness of possibility. Take a deep breath and know that you are strengthened by all your experiences and are now fortified to begin anew.

General:

1. Research how other people cope with similar circumstances.
2. Identify an appropriate use of distraction without going into denial.
3. Read books – anything that interests you.
4. Visit online resources – research what fascinates or heals you.
5. Find relevant support organizations and think about contacting them,
6. Learn something new (language, skill, etc.) ... it jump-starts your thinking and creativity.

Chapter Summary

In this chapter, you reviewed a list of tips that can build your adapting skills. You considered which might be realistic for you and which ideas need further thought. You may even have identified further possibilities for moving forward through adapting.

What's Ahead

You're about to start Part Three: Meaning-Making. In the next chapter, you will learn a definition of meaning-making and the importance of getting out of victim mode. Each of us has the responsibility to choose our response to tragedy, and Chapter 8 discusses ways of doing just that. Have you ever heard of Post Traumatic Growth? Keep reading for new and uplifting ideas.

PART THREE

Meaning-Making

Meaning-Making Creates Possibilities

> "Life is never made unbearable by circumstances, but only by lack of meaning and purpose."
>
> ~ Viktor Frankl

So far, we have discussed accepting our reality, including all the associated thoughts and feelings. We have also looked at adapting to a new situation – how we get used to a new normal.

In this chapter, we will consider the value of meaning-making. We'll reflect on its definition and on the many ways in which we can respond. The idea that we actually have a choice in our response can be both liberating and challenging. We will learn the importance of getting out of victim mode and various categories of meaning-making. Lastly, we will discuss post traumatic growth.

~

When I use the term "meaning-making," I'm talking about the process of understanding or making sense of what's going on in our lives. Many times the meaning of an event seems obviously unquestionable. In the case of bereavement, however, we are often left feeling empty because our dear one's death will never make sense.

Finding meaning in distress can be like turning on a light bulb in a darkened room. Everyone has trouble tolerating meaningless suffering. Yet it can be hard to imagine an explanation for loss, tragedy, or struggle. I believe discovering meaning in challenging circumstances helps us move through these times with greater resilience. It helps us to consider a bigger picture and allow some healing thoughts to mingle with the difficult ones, no matter what life dishes out.

Many times in my life, I've been faced with the challenge of meaning-making. I was 22 when my father died, and I was plagued with the question "Why?" for a long time. Eventually, I concluded there was no reasonable answer, and I needed to stop asking. With each successive loss, I struggled in a different way to make the experience meaningful. But it wasn't until David died that I realized I had a choice.

I could either embrace the randomness of the accident and, thereby, yield to the notion that life is utterly haphazard and always potentially wounding – or I could create some kind of meaning that challenged me to develop a better version of myself. For most of my life, I'd had a front-row seat to the pain and suffering of losing people I loved. Friends commented that they didn't know anyone else who had been through the deaths of so many people close to them. That didn't exactly help me feel any better. It did make me wonder if there was a pattern in my life – that maybe if I worked hard enough, I'd define some sort of redeeming lesson in all the pain.

In his seminal book *Man's Search for Meaning*, Viktor Frankl considered the usefulness of what he called tragic optimism. (In addition to believing that the quest for meaning is key to mental health and human thriving, he spent 3 years during World War II in four different concentration camps.) After telling his story of surviving the Holocaust, he posed the question: "How can life retain its potential meaning in spite of its tragic aspects?" (p. 137)

He noted that we must have reasons to be happy; we can't just demand of ourselves automatic happiness. Frankl maintained this is done through "actualizing the potential meaning inherent and dormant in a given situation." (p. 138). This means thinking of the possible meaning in any single situation; not necessarily trying to come up with the meaning of life as a whole.

This is important, because Frankl is not stating that unhappiness is excused by being an unlucky victim, having random accidents, or being in the wrong place at the wrong time. He is challenging each of us to choose how we respond to any burden. He wrote that, in addition to having the freedom to choose our response, we also have the responsibility to transcend suffering by dedicating ourselves to someone or something else with hope and positive energy. Reading his words felt like he was speaking directly to me.

Frankl identified three paths toward meaning-making: 1) creating a work or doing a deed; 2) experiencing something or encountering someone; and 3) turn a personal tragedy into a triumph. In the case of path #3, he observed, "even the helpless victim of a hopeless situation, facing a fate he cannot change, may rise above himself, may grow beyond himself, and by so doing change himself." (p. 146).

Can anyone turn a predicament into an achievement? Yes, according to Frankl's book. It takes being able to adopt an attitude of benefiting from a traumatic experience (tragic optimism) and seeing it as a growth experience.

Conversely, we don't need to suffer in order to discover meaning. We can make meaning of any situation, even uplifting ones. Frankl maintained that meaning is simply *available* through suffering, provided that the suffering is unavoidable. This essential aspect – unavoidability – is what powers our choice of response through meaning-making.

This was the call to action I needed. Witnessing and experiencing inescapable suffering and death for so many years left me with a yearning to create something positive – to craft order out of chaos. And when David died I took it as a personal mandate – okay, I finally got it – to turn tragedy into triumph by helping others through loss.

Our Cognitive Lives

Trauma and loss can shatter our core beliefs about ourselves and the world we live in. It may force us to seriously re-examine these principles as we attempt to make sense of what happened. Such a reexamination requires a lot of thought, and it turns out there are two kinds.

Event-related *intrusive* rumination is automatic, unwanted musing about the crisis. It tends to occur immediately afterward and is associated with ongoing distress.

Event-related *deliberate* rumination (reflection) tends to lead to constructive ideas and is associated more with growth. It should be noted that intrusive rumination can stimulate future deliberate reflection. (Triplett, K. N.,

Tedeschi, R. G., Cann, A., Calhoun, L. G., & Reeve, C. L. (2011, July 4). Posttraumatic Growth, Meaning in Life, and Life Satisfaction in Response to Trauma. Psychological Trauma: Theory, Research, Practice, and Policy. Advance online publication. doi: 10.1037/a0024204.)

As you consider the content of your own thoughts, try not to judge all intrusive rumination as bad and deliberate reflection as good. Both are typical during the grieving process. Just notice what's there, and pay attention to any shifts over time.

Categories of Meaning-Making

There are many strategies people use for meaning-making, and they're often grouped into various categories, including personal growth and lifestyle changes, spirituality, family bonds, philanthropy, and release from suffering.

Sometimes, losing a loved one makes us value life even more. We try to cherish all the aspects of our existence, which may even lead to finding a new purpose or changing one's lifestyle. These are examples of how grief can lead to meaningful personal growth.

Meaning-making through spirituality can help people cope with loss, and develop our beliefs as we consider inspirational possibilities. Some may use their connection with the divine to cultivate a conviction that the loss is part of God's plan or, conversely, that they're being punished by God. Others may question God's ability to intervene at all. If you don't hold a formally religious perspective, you might create stories about how the universe works.

Changing our outlook toward, and interactions with, family members is another way we might create meaning in loss. Perhaps we spend more time with them and talk about our loved one's legacy. The family feels united as tension and disagreement decrease. In the throes of grief, clinging to and feeling grateful for family can be healing.

Philanthropic and charitable activities are also useful meaning-making strategies. Not only do they create financial support for the chosen organization, but they also enhance social and emotional support for the bereaved. Many people say it turns the difficult experience of death into something life affirming and positive for others.

Post Traumatic Growth

Post Traumatic Growth, or PTG, refers to the positive psychological changes that may be experienced from struggling with a major life crisis or traumatic circumstances. It's actually possible not only to bounce back from great difficulty but to ultimately grow from it.

This phenomenon was discovered and named by researchers Richard Tedeschi and Lawrence Calhoun from the University of North Carolina at Charlotte. Their Post Traumatic Growth Inventory was first published in 1996, and since then, they (and a host of other researchers) have concluded that Post Traumatic Growth is a widespread phenomenon

Areas of Positive Change in PTG

Tedeschi and Calhoun observed that Post traumatic growth tends to occur in five general areas. Sometimes people who face major life crises develop a sense that **new opportunities** have appeared, opening up possibilities that didn't exist before. Secondly, some people experience **closer relationships** with certain people or an increased sense of connection to others who similarly suffer. A third area of possible change is a **realization of one's own strength** – "if I got through that, I can handle anything." Fourth, is a **greater appreciation for life** in general. The fifth area of growth involves **spirituality** or religion. Some experience a deepening of their spirituality that may even herald a significant change in their belief system.

Does this mean we can transform tragic circumstances into happiness? That depends on your definition of happiness. Jim Hendon, in his book *Upside*, describes two types of happiness. He describes hedonic happiness as being associated with the pursuit of pleasure and the avoidance of pain. He notes this type of happiness may be fun but can also be fleeting and lacking in purpose. Hendon goes on to describe eudaimonia, which is a deeper kind of happiness and connected to the pursuit of personal growth and becoming a better person. He states this is much closer to the experience of people who report post traumatic growth.

I believe there is a powerful link between Viktor Frankl's writings on meaning-making and today's research on post traumatic growth. To me, Dr. Frankl is an example of post traumatic growth, even though the words didn't exist then to describe his experience that way.

I also believe that the transformation of post traumatic growth is possible for everyone if we are willing to discover/find/create meaning and adopt tragic optimism. If Frankl could return to life, I would love to introduce him to Tedeschi and Calhoun. What a conversation that would be!

To be sure, not everyone experiences a positive transformation in the aftermath of trauma. But just knowing it's possible (and apparently has always been possible) opens up encouraging potential and maybe even new attitudes. We each get to choose the various aspects of meaning we ascribe to any situation.

Chapter Summary

In this chapter, you have learned a working definition of meaning-making and why it's important in healthy grieving. You have considered Viktor Frankl's concept of "tragic optimism" and have recognized the burden of choice we have in selecting our responses to traumatic loss. You've discovered the categories of meaning-making and the perhaps novel idea of post traumatic growth.

What's Ahead

In the next chapter, we'll consider examples of meaning-making. Some are my own stories, and others are taken from my research. All are meant to inspire your own creative thinking. I, personally, couldn't tolerate the emptiness of meaningless loss. So in the absence of any absolute answers, I decided to create my own significance narratives. Turn the page for inspiring stories of meaning-making.

Stories of Meaning-Making

> "Ultimately, man should not ask what the meaning of his life is, but rather must recognize that it is he who is asked. In a word, each man is questioned by life; and he can only answer to life by answering for his own life; to life he can only respond by being responsible."
>
> ~Viktor Frankl

Now that we know the importance of meaning-making in the grief process, let's consider some examples. This chapter includes some of my own attempts to create meaning as well as stories told to me by others during interviews, sessions, and in questionnaires. I have intentionally omitted all names and other identifying information.

~

My father died after a long battle with cancer when I was 22. He was a beloved physician in our community, and it didn't make sense to me that medical science had no cure for him. I drove myself a little crazy constantly wondering why he had to die so young, especially after helping so many other people. Hadn't he prepaid his ticket to a long life?

By the time my son died, I had spent decades mulling over (at various times) the whys of life and death. There were still no definitive answers. For a long while, I told myself "there are no answers." This was satisfying in the sense that I could stop asking why if I was never going to find "because…"

After David died, I read books written by other bereaved parents and learned that nearly all of them developed some kind of spiritual belief about their child's ongoing existence. This made sense to me, as it was incomprehensible to think that David's energy simply ceased to exist, and I was looking for ways to feel connected to him. All the authors (parents) spoke of finding ways to continue their relationship with their children, even after death. I know…sounds wacky.

Many grievers have consulted mediums. All the advice I've gleaned from my own research points to the same truth: do whatever feels right for you and don't think you have to justify it. One parent's recommendation: "If you're curious and want to see a psychic or medium, research them well; don't go to a fake; there's nothing wrong with wanting to connect. And if you don't feel the need to do that, it's okay too."

From a widow: "My husband was a veteran of the Vietnam War ... The added comfort was not only being with people who are also experiencing a loss but also of being with veterans or spouses of veterans. It felt like a family. I also went to the library and read every book I could get my hands on regarding death, grieving, and the afterlife. Educating myself and understanding as well as indulging in the thought that his spirit is still here took some of the edge off the pain,"

For me, the idea took hold in my brain, and I found myself fascinated by various afterlife theories. I read as much as I could, noting what resonated and what didn't. I realized that *because no one has ever died and returned to report accurate details of the long-term experience*, no one really knows. Therefore, I have (and each of us has) the freedom to choose what I want to believe. What's more, I also have the freedom to change my mind, to modify my beliefs as time goes on. And so my thoughts on what death might be like for David and where he is now have continued to evolve. This freedom to consider various possibilities has felt healing to me.

The Last Train Home

Shortly after David's death, I became interested in afterlife theories. It just didn't seem possible to me that he could be so full of life energy one moment and suddenly cease to exist the next. I devoured books and searched the internet to learn what others think about what happens after death.

In the process, I learned that most bereaved parents have some version of this need to know their child is okay, *somewhere,* and that the love they shared will somehow continue. That's powerful motivation to open up one's ideas about what's possible. With my passion thus normalized, I carried on in earnest.

One notion that resonated was that of a life contract. This assumes that before birth, and with guidance, we all write and agree to key life experiences in order to accomplish our spiritual goals. Included in every contract are five potential exit points and the understanding that one will be used to end that life. Obviously, no one remembers their own contract negotiations or any of the details they approved, including possible exit points.

I constructed a story in my mind in which David had long ago agreed to a short life this time. Perhaps his spirit was that of my beloved father, who died so young from cancer. I imagined him trying to convince the panel of spirit guides to let him return to my life 11 years later, and their stipulation that this lifetime could only complete his earlier, abbreviated one. Adding 26 years on earth now to the 59 years as my father equals a respectable 85 year lifetime. That felt meaningful.

I thought about David having five potential exit points in only 26 years and tried to identify times when he either had a close call or serendipitously avoided possible calamity. Shockingly, I was able to recognize four other such times. In a rush of insight, I could accept his need (unrecognized, though, at the time) to access the last available exit portal of his lifetime. That too felt important.

Obviously, no one really knows what death is like or what truly happens after we die. This "not knowing" affords each of us the opportunity to construct our own meaningful stories based on our individual circumstances and needs.

I felt comforted to believe that David had a hand in choosing his lifetime, even if he got caught up in the excitement and forgot about getting ready for an early departure.

I imagine him suddenly hearing the conductor calling "All Aboard!" and realizing he had to get to the station and locate the right track. And then, I imagine him seated and catching his breath, relieved to have made it, even though a bit disoriented. And although I will always miss him, it's deeply meaningful to think my son caught the last train home.

My Most Unexpected Mother's Day Gift

I hadn't been looking forward to Mother's Day. Don't get me wrong, I'm incredibly grateful for my loving daughters, my miraculous grandsons, and my amazing granddaughters. It's just that I also miss my son, and I feel his absence profoundly on this day that celebrates the mother/child bond. As is my way of coping, I'd already started thinking about how I'd create a meaningful observance of this bittersweet (for me) holiday.

Every bereaved mother I've ever talked with or read about has some type of belief in a spiritual afterlife. It doesn't matter one's religion or background; we mothers seem to cling to the notion that our relationships with our beloved children must somehow continue. It seems incomprehensible that a connection so intense could really be broken or that love's energy would simply cease to exist.

And so, like a host of grieving mothers before me, I began looking for signs I could interpret as clues to David's otherworldly existence and his attempts to communicate with me. I know ... it sounds way out there ... too "woo-woo" for many. That's okay. I've chosen to embrace certain ideas that feel healing and meaningful to me, especially when there's no way to prove them true or false.

Starting shortly after his death, the light in our curio cabinet would go on by itself. I thought at first maybe someone else had turned it on and then considered perhaps there was a short in the wiring. Never finding an explanation, I decided to view it as a friendly hello from David.

At various times of the day and night throughout the first 18 months after his death, the light surprisingly came on. Its brightness never failed to lift my mood as I imagined his presence in the room with me.

And then it stopped.

I tested the touch-switch, and it worked just fine. I told myself it didn't mean anything and to be patient; to quit reading anything into it. Despite my reasonable self-talk, however, an unmistakable loneliness settled over me as more months rolled by.

One night, I decided to ask David directly to send me a sign that he was around and okay. The thought went out into the evening silence as love and longing welled up in my heart. Then I closed my eyes and went to sleep.

A week later, I received an email offering me free tickets to a Chicago play called The Pianist of Willesden Lane. I read the plot summary:

"Set in Vienna in 1938 and in London during the Blitzkrieg, The Pianist of Willesden Lane tells the true story of Mona Golabek's mother, noted pianist and author Lisa Jura. A young Jewish pianist, Lisa dreams of a concert debut at the storied Musikverein concert hall. When Lisa is sent on the Kindertransport to London to protect her from the Nazi regime, everything about her life is upended except her love of music and her pursuit of her dream. Golabek performs some of the world's most beloved piano music in the poignant true story of her mother's experience in wartime Europe."

Without knowing how I came to receive this offer, I was drawn to the play's themes. My own mother, who died in 1991 after a long battle with emphysema, had been a gifted pianist and played nightly concerts for us in the secure privacy of our home. She struggled with debilitating anxiety and panic attacks for as long as I can remember. Who knows what she might have accomplished had she been able to overcome her angst? I always felt disconnected from her and strove to be as different a woman as I could be.

As I sat in the darkened theater the night of the performance, however, I began to experience my mother in a new way. She would have been only slightly older than the play's teenage heroine during World War II and possessed a similar passion for classical piano. I wondered what it was like for her as a young American Jewish woman to learn about Nazi atrocities when the war was over. I thought about her reunion with her handsome young husband (my father) when he returned from overseas after their two-year separation.

As familiar, evocative melodies swirled through the auditorium and my being, I felt a powerful connection to my mother through the music and an empathy I could never have imagined. With tear-stained cheeks and a lump in my throat, I finally realized my mother was so much more than the frightened woman who raised me. She was also a talented, passionate artist who bestowed many gifts that I am only now beginning to open.

I've thought about this experience a lot since it happened. How did my name come to be on an email distribution list for free tickets? Why this particular play? Why now? I'll never know. Therefore, I take it as an opportunity to believe something meaningful.

I imagine my beloved David, together with my misunderstood mother, illuminating my place among the generations. I envision them presenting me with a most unexpected and profound Mother's Day gift: eternal love that spans time and place and connects us all.

Memorials and Legacies

Each year, I mark my son's birthday by honoring someone else. My intention was to connect something positive to the day and to David's legacy, so we established a memorial leadership award at the company where he worked. With the help of their administrative team, we identified several core strengths he embodied, and these became the criteria by which award nominees would be considered. The recipient, selected from among peer nominees, best demonstrates the leadership qualities that David embodied. In an attempt to make David's birthday an ongoing celebration of his life, we agreed to present the award each year on that exact date, Oct. 25th (or as close to it as possible). It feels heartwarming and healing to gather with the entire company to celebrate both my son's legacy and those who carry it on.

Each year the list of nominees has grown as more people notice and value their colleagues' work ethic and kindness. This has been very meaningful to me.

Similarly, parents whose children have died from brain tumors have found helping others very meaningful. Some have launched nonprofit fundraisers benefiting the American Brain Tumor Association, while others have become parent mentors with the Pediatric Brain Tumor Foundation.

Transformation

Sometimes, one of the outcomes of grief is discovering who we are without our loved ones who have died. People report noticing they have become more compassionate and patient than they were previously; that they have gained a deeper appreciation for life, people, and love that they didn't have before.

In the words of a grieving mother: "I hope you become more mindful and grateful for the positive things in life and for the beauty that surrounds you. I know that for me and for many of my friends who are also bereaved parents, we have all become more that way."

A bereaved friend described realizing that although her confidante was no longer alive, she was still a connection to a profound stream of wisdom that could be tapped at will. This wisdom stream keeps their bond thriving.

Chapter Summary

This chapter has provided a more personal view of meaning-making. You have read accounts of my own meaning choices and those of others, many of which relate to spirituality. They are not meant to imply you should adopt any of these views. Rather, the stories are included to inspire your own search for meaningful possibilities.

What's Ahead

As in previous sections, our discussion of meaning-making will conclude with a chapter on skill-building. You will read thought prompts and questions to open up your thinking about meaning creation. You can use these inquiries for journaling, meditation, discussion, or just to think about. Read on to find meaning in your personal situation.

———◆——◆———

Meaning-Making Skill-Building Tips

> "Each man must look to himself to teach him the meaning of life. It is not something discovered: it is something molded."
>
> ~ Antoine de Saint-Exupery

Here, in Chapter 10, I offer ideas for building your own meaning-making skills while facing the death of someone you love. As always, there are no wrong answers; the plan is to stimulate your thinking in order to identify some personally meaningful thoughts.

Here is a list of questions and action items that can help illuminate the meaning in difficult situations. These thought prompts are not original; they come from various websites, books, and conversations over the years.

If you keep a journal, you might write your responses there. You might also use these as meditation prompts or discussion questions (hopefully, with people who are open, supportive, and nonjudgmental). Or just contemplate whatever comes up when you read each question. Your thoughts may change and develop over time, so don't hesitate to occasionally revisit the list.

1. Is there meaning in this loss? During my most agonizingly bereft moments, I just couldn't accept that David was gone in a split second for no apparent reason. I eventually decided to create a meaning that worked for me. As individuals, we get to choose our own.

2. What lessons can be learned from this experience? Whenever something negative happens, I always ask myself what I can learn from it. Sometimes the answer is obvious, and other times I have to make up something. But it always requires a certain amount of self-reflection that is ultimately beneficial.

3. What self-discoveries am I making? This kind of inquiry can reveal so many things about ourselves: how we tend to function under adverse conditions, how we relate to others, or what effect this is having on mood, thoughts,

energy, and behavior. It's important to notice the Self.

4. What personal qualities have been strengthened? Perhaps there's something in your make-up that has been quietly in the background until now...something that has responded to a call to action of sorts. Maybe it's tenacity, appreciation, gentleness, or a host of other possibilities. Look carefully.

5. What strengths can I identify that were not apparent before? Even though I would never choose such a loss, I do recognize now a certain resilience that I never would have thought possible. It was cultivated through trial and error, but it's now mine forever. What new strengths are you noticing?

6. What is becoming of the person I used to be? We all evolve over time, and sometimes life transitions hasten that evolution. Sometimes we have no choice but to change, and it's important to honor our past selves before we let them go.

7. Who am I now? This is a big question and not always easy to answer. Take your time. I had to add "bereaved mother" to my response, and at first, it was my only focus. In time, I could broaden my answer to include all my other aspects as well.

8. What was important to me before this loss compared to what is important now? Have

certain longings and stressors faded into the background? Or are there people and things you took for granted that are now at the top of your list? Think about the difference in what's important to you now.

9. How has this experience impacted my values and/or spiritual beliefs? Most of us don't talk about these thoughts very often, but this may be the perfect time to consider them. Keep an open mind as you reflect on your views. Again, don't be surprised if this continues to evolve.

10. Do I see the world any differently now? Life experience can certainly change our outlook, so it makes sense to contemplate how recent challenges may have altered our perception. It may be a subtle shift, a global transformation, or something in between.

11. Make note of your automatic ruminations for 24 hours. These are thoughts that come into your awareness with no planning or intention. Make note of your deliberate reflections for 24 hours. These are ideas you want to consider and mull over.

12. Repeat the above exercise each month and see if there's a difference.

13. How have my personal relationships changed?

14. Consider helping someone else. Some people find supporting others through similar challenges actually lifts them out of their own despair.

15. Consider some type of memorial that is meaningful to you. Figure out possible ways of starting and maintaining it.

16. Explore spiritual inspirations and consider adopting whatever fits for you. It doesn't matter whether it's prayer, affirmations, or a new belief. There's no right or wrong when it comes to one's personal spirituality.

17. Ask yourself if it's possible to grow from what you have been through. Not that you would ever be glad this loss happened, but as long as it did, are there ways you have grown?

Chapter Summary

In this chapter, you have considered many existential questions that are meant to inspire further thinking. This is a lot to take in during an initial reading so keep pondering and working (or playing around) with any ideas that are meaningful to you. There are no "shoulds;" just possibilities.

What's Ahead

You are about to embark on the fourth facet of grief: replenishing. This can be challenging for many who are used to back-burnering their own needs. But self-care is important, and the next chapter answers the question: Is

Self-Care Selfish? Turn the page for an intriguing discussion.

PART FOUR

Replenishing

Replenishing Body, Mind, and Spirit

"Rest and self-care are so important. When you take time to replenish your spirit, it allows you to serve others from the overflow. You cannot serve from an empty vessel."

~ Eleanor Brownn; eleanorbrownn.com

Are you ready to replenish? In this chapter, we discuss the benefits of self-care and why it's especially important during the stress of grieving. You will learn why self-care is definitely not selfish (in the traditional sense of the word) and a few different types of self-care. The chapter concludes by introducing the concept of depleters and replenishers.

~

Is Self-Care Selfish?

Let's look at the word "selfish." It has a negative connotation of someone who *only* cares about him- or herself. But what if we thought of the Self (with a capital S) as the essential part of our being that distinguishes us from others. Pretty special, huh?

It seems reasonable to take really good care of something you possess that is special. In that sense, we all need to be Selfish. I'm not advocating narcissism or not caring about others; I'm just allowing for reasonable ways to cherish and nurture the unique human that each of us certainly is.

When you have a physical wound or illness, people will tell you to take care of yourself. They expect you to do what the doctor says in order to heal and get back to a state of wellness. And it makes sense to follow those directions – rest, eat healthfully, do whatever it takes to recover.

But having another kind of wound, as in grieving, is a different story altogether. No one can tell from the outside how badly we're hurting; our suffering is mostly hidden, and we appear just fine. We even try hard to do all the regular stuff of life – working, shopping, exercising – so no one can tell what's happening on the inside.

Grieving is the human response to loss – any loss. It's how we heal from this particular kind of hurt, and it makes sense. Therefore, it also makes sense to take extra good care of ourselves while we grieve.

Different Kinds of Self-Care

The most obvious way to care for ourselves is to make sure we're physically healthy. In early grief, I advise everyone to get a regular check-up with their health care provider and to see their dentist. Stress can have a negative effect on the immune system, so it makes sense to reasonably monitor our physical wellness.

This is also the time to make sure you're eating as healthily as you can and that you're sleeping well, regularly. If eating or sleeping is difficult for more than two weeks, see your doctor. It's also important to pay attention to moving your body. If you like to exercise, do what you enjoy. Otherwise, make sure you walk or do some kind of movement that's appropriate for you each day. This is also something to discuss with your health care provider.

Emotional self-care is also important. Pay attention to your mood, thoughts, feelings, and behavior, noting if anything seems "off" or concerns you or those you're closest to. Meeting with a therapist or counselor can help you monitor your emotional life and develop effective coping strategies. Talking with friends can also be useful, but make sure they are nonjudgmental and don't have an agenda for you.

No one can go through grief without feeling sad, angry, annoyed, tired, and a host of other thoughts and emotions that come up unbidden. All of these are normal and to be expected. Time and support will lessen their intensity, and you'll gradually find a new way of navigating reality. Reach out for help and support if you feel stuck in your misery.

The third type of self-care is spiritual. Be aware of what thoughts, ideas, practices, and surroundings make you feel connected to something larger than yourself. For some, this may refer to religious beliefs and customs. To others, it might describe how you feel when in nature, meditating, or doing yoga, for example. Many find a combination of these works well.

People seek spirituality for many reasons. Some people want to find meaning in life, a connection to something greater than themselves, inspiration to improve themselves, or answers to how life works. Others are searching for happiness, release from suffering, enlightenment, or support for making a difference.

There is no right or wrong when it comes to spiritual self-care. You get to decide what spirit means to you and how you prefer to meet those needs. It can be (and often is) an ongoing process over time. Explore and notice what feels healing to you.

Why is Self-Care Important?

Taking good care of your Self makes the other three facets of grieving (accepting, adapting, and meaning-making) possible. When self-care is absent or inadequate, you likely feel depleted. That's no way to approach the high energy demands of grieving.

Feeling replenished in body, mind, and spirit helps you to fully acknowledge your reality. You can tell your story and express your feelings about it without being constantly overwhelmed and crushed.

A replenished Self can also more skillfully adapt to new circumstances even when they're undesirable. Your creativity and problem-solving ability will be much more obvious when your entire being feels well nourished.

And it is much easier to find or create meaning in challenging situations when every aspect of your individuality feels supported. You may more readily find inspiration as you consider different possibilities.

Put Your Oxygen Mask on First

Every flight attendant on every airplane I've ever flown offers the same advice: put your oxygen mask on first, before helping others. Why? Obviously, we wouldn't be very effective helpers if we're not okay ourselves. The same is true regarding the grief process: we aren't effective grievers if we're completely depleted, either. Make sure your oxygen mask is firmly in place. Here are some useful strategies to consider. More ideas are in Chapter 13: Replenishing Action Items.

Mindfulness Meditation

There are many ways to meditate, but one method is to sit quietly for a few minutes focusing on your breath. Inevitably, you'll have random thoughts, and as soon as you're aware of the shift in concentration, return to your breathing. Remember not to judge the content of your thoughts or how quickly you resume paying attention to your breath.

You don't have to sit in any particular position or subscribe to any belief system in order to meditate. It's also not necessary to sit for any prescribed amount of time; some beginners start with a one-minute meditation. It may sound simple, but it can be quite challenging to keep returning to a single focus.

Scientific research suggests mindfulness meditation can lower stress hormones, reduce blood pressure, and boost the immune system. It can also ease depression, anxiety, ADHD, and some types of cognitive decline.

Emotional Freedom Techniques (EFT or "Tapping")

EFT is often described as a combination of ancient acupressure and modern psychology. It got its nickname "tapping" because you tap your body's meridian points (mostly on the head and upper body) while using precise language to illuminate and resolve various aspects of a particular problem.

Anyone can learn EFT, and there are many practitioners who can work with you to enhance your skills. It can be beneficial to work with a therapist to reconcile the thoughts, memories, and feelings that often arise in the process.

Research studies show the brain's fight-or-flight reaction and the body's stress response can be reduced by stimulating these meridian points (as in acupuncture). Further research indicates that light pressure – as is used in tapping – is enough to produce the same results. Needle-free emotional acupuncture!

Gratitude

Appreciating the good things in life has real benefits. It brings forth positive emotions, which in turn, start a cascade of mental, physical, and spiritual benefits. Life's difficulties begin to shift from center-stage to, maybe, somewhere in the orchestra pit. You know the musicians are there, and they certainly shape the production. Sometimes, the orchestra even rises into full view. But it always recedes again so you can pay attention to the main characters.

So it is with gratitude; it helps you pay more attention to life's gifts while maintaining awareness of its challenges. In fact, the gifts may be even more meaningful precisely because of these challenges and the perspective they provide. Gratitude is *not* acting as if everything is always wonderful.

Some people choose to cultivate a daily gratitude practice in which they think of three things they're grateful for every day. Some keep these lists in a journal; others just pause to reflect. Further ideas are noted in Chapter 13: Replenishing Action Items.

Balance Connection and Solitude

Each of us has our own individual needs for alone time and for being with others. It's important during grieving to honor those needs, which may be different than they were previously.

Pay attention to your shifting wishes to be with specific people from your support network and to spend time by yourself. Find your own balance; it may not necessarily be equal. Even though a certain amount of solitude can be replenishing, be careful not to isolate yourself completely.

Depleters and Replenishers

Navigating loss and grief is not easy. It's common to become depleted by events, people, and even your own emotions. I refer to such events, people, and emotions as depleters, acknowledging that sometimes we see them coming and other times they take us by surprise.

The antidote to depletion is replenishing, but what feels replenishing to me might not to you. So it's wise to develop a running list of your own personal replenishers to use before, during, and after difficult moments.

Think of all the experiences that evoke the "ahhhh" response for you. This would include anything that makes you feel relaxed, serene, and peaceful. Some strategies might be easily accessible and free (taking a warm bath or listening to your favorite music), while others require an appointment and cost money (a massage or manicure). I do not recommend alcoholic beverages to be among anyone's replenishers.

When you feel depleted by an experience, put one of your replenishers in place as soon as you can. If you know ahead of time that you're going into a depleting (or potentially depleting) event, plan your replenisher in advance. You might even choose a replenishing activity before and after a depleting occasion, which I call a "replenisher sandwich."

Chapter Summary

In this chapter, you have considered the benefits of self-care and why this is especially important during the grief process. You may have a new perspective on the word "selfish" as you think about what your Self needs to thrive. You have learned about different kinds of self-care, including meditation, tapping, gratitude, and balancing connection with solitude. Lastly, you understand the value of replenishing yourself when you become depleted.

What's Ahead

Chapter 12: Stories of Replenishing will give you a greater sense of what replenishing looks and feels like. You will read how I have strengthened my sense of self-worth and given myself permission to feel moments of joy even in sorrow. I discuss how to be hopeful when things seem hopeless and my experiences of observing nature and being with my grandchildren. Let's turn now to these illustrations of replenishing.

Stories of Replenishing

> "When you recover or discover something that nourishes your soul and brings joy, care enough about yourself to make room for it in your life."
>
> ~ Jean Shinoda Bolen

This chapter illustrates various kinds of replenishing. You will learn how I strengthened my self-worth and gave myself permission to feel moments of joy even when I was in the midst of sorrow. I also discuss how to be hopeful even when things seem hopeless and give specific examples of my personal replenishing experiences.

I am often asked how it's possible to take really good care of yourself when you don't quite believe you're worth it.

A great question, because most people I know feel that way at some point in their lives. Individually, a therapist can help you understand how your thoughts and feelings about yourself may have taken hold in childhood and how they have evolved over the years.

But there are also some general concepts that I've used to turn "selfish" into "healing self-care."

Seven Steps to Boosting My Own Self- Worth

1. I made a list of all my thoughts and beliefs about myself, then I noted whether each one was positive, negative, or neutral.
2. I tried to be positive and forgiving with myself as I scanned my list, even if I could only do that for this exercise.
3. I appreciated and savored all the positive thoughts and beliefs that were on my list.
4. I tried not to compare myself with anyone else.
5. I challenged all the negative beliefs or inaccurate thoughts by asking myself, "Really?" (I'm a terrible friend because I never make phone calls ... really?)
6. I adjusted my thoughts and beliefs to reflect a more realistic and supportive approach. (I'm a loving, low-maintenance friend who prefers face-to-face visits over phone calls.)
7. I looked in the mirror and smiled. I gave myself a truly loving smile, accepting the total package of

all my strengths and limitations. No, I'm not perfect; no one is. There is a lot I can still work on. But basically, I'm okay and worthy of love.

I noticed after doing this exercise once that my list had changed. I was able to identify more neutral or positive self-thoughts than previously. Over time, and many more iterations, I found myself letting go of old mantras that were no longer ringing true.

Permission to Feel Joy: How I Access Positive Feelings

After a tragedy or serious life challenge, it's understandable to believe you can never be truly happy again. Here's what I did to nourish myself and allow some mini-doses of healing.

Identify Opposing Feelings

Over time, I realized that in addition to feeling heartbroken over my son's death, I was also noticing other feelings rambling around in my mind. I was grateful for my close friends and family who took such good care of me. I was happy to have memories, pictures, and videos of David through all the years of his life. I was surprised to be completely and wonderfully distracted for two hours sitting through a movie at my local theater. I even found myself laughing out loud playing with my grandsons! How was it possible to be so devastated and yet have other feelings at the same time? Was there something wrong with me?

No, there was absolutely nothing wrong with me! I was noticing the human capacity to have more than one feeling at the same time. In the example above, I identified a particular feeling attached to a certain experience. Although I noticed my tendency to alternate between loss-related feelings and distraction-enabled feelings, the truth is that I often sensed both simultaneously.

Acknowledge Different Parts of Self

It is also useful to cultivate an awareness of different parts of ourselves. There was a part of me that was profoundly sad all the time. This part seemed inconsolable and always at least in the background. There was another part of me that felt angry at the unfairness of the situation. And yet another part of me was overwhelmingly joyful to have my wonderful daughter and precious grandsons nearby.

We all have the ability to decide which feelings get our attention. It's okay to send uncomfortable feelings into the background for a while and enjoy the healing of positive states. This is not denial; it's needed respite, and a form of self-care. It's also okay to focus on sorrow when you're ready to have a good cry. A healthy, balanced inner life is ours for the choosing.

Replenishing the Body (Which Affects Mind and Spirit)

I have long known that I feel better when I walk a lot. I function better on days when I incorporate walking into my schedule, and it doesn't matter whether it's on a treadmill, in nature, or just doing errands. Now that we're told we should all be walking 10 thousand steps a day, I have another reason to get going. I bought myself a fitness tracker bracelet and sure enough, the more steps I log, the better I feel.

Paying attention to my sleep has also been useful, and my fitness tracker records that too (time awake, asleep, and restless). Sleep hygiene refers to habits and practices that promote sleeping well on a regular basis so I couldn't ignore how hard it was to sleep well after my son died.

One strategy I tried was to go to bed and wake up at approximately the same time every day, regardless of my actual schedule. Another useful step is not to alter my sleep cycle by more than 15 minutes at any one time.

To this day, Sundays are difficult sleep-nights for me, and I either have trouble falling asleep or staying asleep. I have learned not to fight this phenomenon – it's part of my grieving. I get up and find something quietly relaxing to do until I'm feeling sleepy again.

Another physical experience that has always felt replenishing to me in so many ways is getting a manicure and/or pedicure. Besides leaving with beautiful nails, I feel profoundly cared for in the process.

Body-Mind-Spirit Practices

Yoga has long been one of my favorite exercise routines, precisely because it also benefits my mood as well. I have, at various times, taken yoga classes at fitness centers, studios, and at retreats. I've also developed a home practice with the help of online classes.

Qi Gong is another such practice that also keeps our energy moving healthfully. I enjoy these routines during indoor and outdoor classes, and sometimes I select an online video to follow at home.

EFT, or "Tapping," has been a favorite routine for many years. It consists of tapping on a prescribed set of points on your own body while verbally acknowledging your thoughts and feelings with specific statements. It teaches your system to relax while stressed, which in turn, allows meaningful healing. I have used tapping to calm my own overwhelming shock, sadness, and stress of grieving.

Mindfulness meditation has long been a replenishing practice for me. Sometimes I meditate for only a few minutes; other sessions are longer. But I always feel rejuvenated by the break from mental busyness.

How to be Hopeful Even When Things Seem Hopeless

There are times when it feels impossible to be hopeful. Or even silly and misguided to go there. But wouldn't it be healing to transform disappointment, grief, sadness and even despair into something positive?

What am I hoping for?

It's important to realistically identify what you're hoping for. There are some things that cannot be changed, no matter how much you wish or how hard you try. It won't do any good to hope that our departed loved ones come back to life or that a challenging situation simply ceases to be. But we *can* hope that our responses to life stress of any kind can improve, thereby helping us to ultimately feel better.

When David died, I spent a lot of time at first wishing it were a terrible nightmare and that I'd soon awaken, overwhelmingly relieved that it wasn't really so. That would have solved everything, but it obviously wasn't realistic. It was agonizing to know my dreams would never come true.

Over time, I realized my Self actually needed something to hope for, even though what I really wanted wasn't possible. So I began a quest to find something achievable to anticipate.

I could hope for the pain to ease... for fewer tears and, someday, more smiles. I hoped for the strength to walk through my grief and for the ability to feel peaceful again. I longed for the day when it would be "old news" and memory would feel like a blessing instead of a curse. Later, I hoped to transform my sorrow into something meaningful that would benefit others.

What is Under My Control?

Another key concept is control or even influence. There are so many difficulties in life that we honestly just can't dictate so yearning for something different may not be a fruitful exercise. However, we can all choose how we'll cope no matter how awful the circumstances.

Part of my healing work included figuring out my choices. When did I want to go back to work? To whom did I want to talk? How much solitude did I need and how much connection? How much distraction was useful and how much focus on what happened? There were endless decisions to be made and what at first felt overwhelming later became helpful proof that there were still any things under my control.

How Can I Help Myself?

Once it's determined where your control is, you can then figure out your own self-care strategies. The obvious ones include getting regular sleep (sometimes easier said than done), healthy eating, exercise, and appropriate medical attention. Each of us also gets to choose activities that are personally replenishing, like being in nature, taking a bubble bath, or enjoying art or music (more examples are in Chapter 13: Replenishing Action Ideas).

Take the time to list everything you find restorative. These are usually centered around the five senses – things you can see, hear, taste, feel, and smell. If a certain type of music, for example, always makes you feel relaxed and soothed, this is the time to bring more of it into your life.

How Can Others Help Me?

Close friends and family members may not know what to say or do, even though they want to help. Don't hesitate to let them know what's useful (and not useful) for you at this time. Of course, this can only be discovered through some thoughtful musing, so give yourself the space to ponder possibilities.

I remember telling people it felt good to hear David's name and to please talk about him. I asked for help acknowledging contributions and gifts of food; I sought out stories from other bereaved parents. And talking with an unbiased, supportive, and nonjudgmental third party is always healing.

Looking Out My Window

My desk at home is near a large window that overlooks a pond and landscaped walking paths. We have lived here long enough for me to appreciate every season, and I am replenished by what I see.

Springtime brings new swans and shortly thereafter, cygnets. Watching them grow to adult size in one year is always astonishing. The fountains are turned on as new buds and flowers decorate the landscape.

Summer shows me the trees and bushes leafed out in a grand display, hiding the far end of the pond. Older people walking slowly; young parents pushing buggies, everyone seems to enjoy meandering along the lake. Families of waterfowl (swans, ducks, and geese) glide across the water, joined by the occasional heron.

Autumn comes ablaze with color and a carpet of leaves. The swans are taken to their winter home, and the fountains are turned off. Even though I can see more branches, the far side of the lake is still hidden by weeping willows.

Winter is a silent but magical time on the pond. Usually blanketed in snow, I can see footprints of various sizes where wildlife has come to visit. The paths are kept clean for hardy winter walkers, and the bare trees allow vistas across the water to a footbridge and connecting lake.

The ever-changing natural beauty of this environment feeds my soul, and I'm sustained by being able to enjoy it through sight, sound (when the windows are open), and touch (on my own neighborhood walks). I am uplifted by my beautiful surroundings.

Spending Time with My Grandchildren

One of my favorite ways to replenish is to be with my grandchildren. They are proof positive that life does indeed go on even when I'm grieving. I feel reassured by their very presence and by the way my heart soars that joy is still possible even in the midst of sadness. And they remind me to stay in the moment, not so concerned with the past or future. It is a treat to enter their world – a place of discovery, wonder, and creativity – as often as possible.

Following Your Passions

Have you ever been engaged in an activity that was so absorbing you lost track of time? For me, it's writing that transcends the here and now. Others run, paint, or make music.

One person fosters orphaned puppies, sometimes taking in entire litters! She raises them until they are ready for adoption, even getting up every two hours to bottle feed them in the first few weeks. She mentioned it can be hard and messy work, but that it has brought her so much joy. And there is no way, she said, to be caught up in grief when you have wiggly puppies who make you laugh and feel joy and unconditional love – completely life affirming!

Chapter Summary

In this chapter, you have reviewed stories of replenishing, which hopefully provide ideas to boost your own sense of renewal. You have read examples of strengthening one's self-worth and allowing moments of joy into the grief process. You also understand how it is possible to access hope in the midst of hopelessness and the value of finding personal replenishers.

What's Ahead

Chapter 13: Replenishing Skill-Building Tips includes more ideas and a 7-step system to discover your personal replenishers. Remember that replenishing is an ongoing process, so be open to adding new possibilities and deleting ones you've tried and don't like. Turn the page to begin your personal replenishing journey.

Replenishing Skill-Building Tips

"I have come to believe that caring for myself is not self indulgent.

Caring for myself is an act of survival."

~ Audre Lorde

In this chapter, you have the opportunity to create your own personal replenishing system. Here are suggestions to jump-start your self-care and a 7-step method to discover your personal replenishers. Because replenishing is an ongoing process, be willing to try new possibilities and scrap ones you don't like. Play around with different ideas and see which ones work for you.

~

It is not selfish to take good care of your Self, especially when you're going through any type of major life stress like loss and grief. It's easy to become depleted by events, people, and even your own emotions.

Since the antidote to depletion is replenishing, here are some action steps you can take to achieve and maintain your highest level of wellbeing.

1. See your health care provider for a check-up.
2. See your dentist for a check-up.
3. Develop a relaxing bedtime ritual.
4. Go for a run, walk, or jog.
5. Work out at a health club.
6. Take a yoga class.
7. Take a qigong class.
8. Meditate
9. Practice EFT or Tapping
10. Work on a coloring book.
11. Make a gratitude list.
12. Gaze into a crackling fire.
13. Cultivate caring and supportive relationships.
14. Explore your past for clues on how you best navigate stress. What have you learned from previous challenges, even if they weren't comparable?
15. Cultivate a positive view of yourself along with confidence in your strengths and abilities.
16. Look for opportunities for self-discovery; learn something new.

17. Become a problem solver and ask what you can learn from any experience.

18. Imagine possibilities.

19. Create your personal replenisher system:

    a. Find a time when you are reasonably relaxed and ready to reflect. Grab your phone, tablet, computer, or even pen and paper – use whatever works best for you. Remember, you're making a list of ideas, which will always be a working document subject to revisions and editing.

    b. Think about your five senses – sight, smell, taste, touch, and hearing. Start with sight and ask yourself what experience reliably brings on the "ahhh" response for you. What do you *love* looking at? Is there an image that evokes love, calm, joy, peace, and serenity every time you see it? It could be photos of loved ones, the ocean at sunset, flowers; it doesn't matter as long as you love looking at it. Note it on your replenisher list.

    c. Go on to the next sense. Smell – is there a fragrance you love? It could be perfume, candles, body lotion, essential oils, or the scent of chocolate chip cookies baking. Add your choices to your list.

    d. Taste – Do you have a favorite food or beverage that always evokes pleasure? People have mentioned mint chocolate chip ice cream, cotton candy, hot cocoa, and watermelon. I do not recommend alcoholic beverages here or overindulging in anything. We're just looking to get to "ahhh." Add these to your list.

e.   Touch – What feels really good? It could be fabric, something in nature, your favorite sofa, petting your dog, or getting a massage. List the things you love to feel that induce relaxation.

f.   Hearing – Certain sounds do have an effect on us. Suggestions here include specific kinds of music, instruments, bird song, wind chimes, waves, and water fountain sounds. Some have included the sound of their best friend's voice. Add your favorites to your list.

g.   Now add activities that combine more than one sense. Include some that are free and can be accessed quickly (taking a candlelight bubble bath, sipping a cup of tea while listening to Mozart, talking with a friend) and some that cost money and may need to be scheduled (a massage, manicure, pedicure, or yoga class).

Chapter Summary

You now have a blueprint for your personal replenishing system as well as a list of skills that are typically rejuvenating and important for wellbeing. Go ahead and create your list of ideas to try, tweaking and modifying as needed.

What's Ahead

You are about to begin Part Five: Synthesizing. The following chapter will help you integrate the 4 Facets of Grief you have been reading about in this book. Accepting, Adapting, Meaning-Making, and Replenishing work together to keep you healthy and able as you navigate the painful challenges of losing someone you love. Keep reading for insight on how to pull these facets together.

PART FIVE

Synthesizing

—◆—

Blending the
Rebuild Your Life

> "Grieving is the act of affirming or reconstructing a personal world of meaning that has been challenged by loss...It requires us to reconstruct a world that again 'makes sense,' ...that restores a semblance of meaning, direction, and interpretability to a life that is forever transformed."
>
> ~ Robert Neimeyer, Ph.D,
> http://www.robertneimeyerphd.com

You now have a framework for transforming your grief. Instead of following a series of steps, you have the freedom to create a process of your own design. You may work with various thoughts, ideas, and strategies as they occur to you, or you might like to use the suggestions presented here.

tory, gemstones and crystals have been possess healing properties. Some believe metaphysical symbolism and search for just ght stone to improve a person's wellbeing.

I think of the 4 Facets described in this book as aspects of another exquisite wonder of the natural world: grief. It's exquisite in the sense of being demanding, challenging, and intense while also moving us toward perspective, renewal, and growth. Since the dawn of mankind, mourning the loss of people we love has been an unavoidable and transformative part of life.

One by one, each of the 4 Facets joins together to generate a radiant new beginning. Accepting the unacceptable brings you face-to-face with reality while Adapting to your new circumstances inspires fresh ideas going forward. Meaning-Making ponders the significance and implications of your loss, and Replenishing ensures your continued self-care.

Despite the pain of emptiness and deprivation, it is possible to have a new goal: reconnecting with joy and building a new life. Applying the 4 Facets helps you enrich your inner resources to feel empowered. You don't move on from your loss; you are always moving through it in evolving ways. Let go of passive victimhood and become a change agent in your own life.

Begin by allowing yourself to feel hopeful. Hope inspires us to keep going no matter how difficult our circumstances may be. We hope for a better day tomorrow; for more comfort and less pain; for meaningful insights and new sources of strength. What are you hoping for in your grief process?

It would be overwhelming to think about and work with all the Facets at the same time, so follow your thoughts and note your focus. Remember, you are the expert on YOU. Some people start with Accepting since the other Facets depend on inhabiting our reality. Then they continue through Adapting, Meaning-Making, and Replenishing in order to become familiar with each Facet. After that initial introduction, you will probably notice how they overlap, blend, expand, and retreat over time. Follow what seems important to you in any given moment and honor it. Your personal journey should be a reflection of the unique, precious, brilliant individual that you are.

I encourage people to track which Facet you may notice during any particular part of a day. Don't worry about forcing an equal focus on all the Facets every day; your natural grief process will find a useful balance for you. The advantage of tracking, however, is that it reminds you to pay attention to any aspect that may have been subconsciously avoided or resisted (usually for valid reasons).

One tracking method is journaling. You can identify the Facets that come into your awareness in any way that works for you. Some like to describe this in great detail while others prefer to jot down bullet points and key phrases. I recommend any system that fits your style.

For those who are interested in a more structured method, I offer two different grief trackers.

The Weekly Grief Tracker offers space to write brief notes relating to each of the Facets. You don't have to list something in every box; just jot down brief details of your thoughts, feelings, or actions as the Facets enter your awareness. You can keep your weekly pages to see how things change over time, stay mindful only of the current week, or even discuss them with your therapist or counselor.

The Monthly Grief Tracker offers a simple check-off method of noting your focus (and fewer pages). Just fill in the date and place a check mark in the box under the corresponding facet. While this provides less detail of your thoughts, feelings, and activities, it does give you a quick visual impression of your grief process throughout the month.

To receive blank copies of both the Weekly and Monthly Grief Trackers via email, go here:
https://app.convertkit.com/landing_pages/248305?v=6

Weekly Grief Tracker

Day	Accepting	Adapting	Meaning Making	Replenishing
Sunday				
Monday				
Tuesday				
Wednesday				
Thursday				
Friday				
Saturday				

Monthly Grief Tracker

Date	Accepting	Adapting	Meaning Making	Replenishing

Any of these tracking methods will help you notice your progress with the 4 Facets. Play around with options that seem reasonable and adopt what works for you.

You may become aware of wanting to discuss your experience of the 4 Facets with other people. One possibility is to talk with a therapist who is well versed in grief and loss, even if they are unfamiliar with the 4 Facets. Some turn to their clergy person or another counselor. Information from your Grief Tracker will be very helpful in communicating your thoughts and feelings to any professional. Please make sure you are speaking with someone who provides unconditional positive regard, is nonjudgmental, and does not have an agenda for you.

Sometimes it is validating to connect with bereaved friends, relatives, or acquaintances. They understand perhaps better than anyone what it's like to grieve. At the same time, pay attention to your gut feelings because such connections can also become overwhelming. Bereavement support groups are many and varied, and their usefulness depends on the facilitator, the make-up and structure of the given group, and your needs at the moment.

Through it all, remember that you are a beautiful, precious, and unrepeatable miracle who deserves to be happy. Perhaps the journey through loss really is like the cutting, honing, and polishing of a gemstone. Even though it requires commitment and sustained effort, it transforms nature's raw material into a pure and radiant jewel ... whole, multifaceted, and inspiring. I believe this is possible for us all.

About the Author

Ruth E. Field, LCSW is that rare expert who offers both knowledge and true empathy.

As a therapist and bereaved mother, daughter, sister, aunt, and friend, she uniquely combines her professional social work training and expertise with her personal experience as a heartbroken family member. She understands grief and loss from the inside out.

Having transformed her own sorrow into a personal mission to help others, she believes strongly in the power of resilience, and that it can be learned. She also considers the grieving process to be effective in navigating other types of loss as well, and is dedicated to teaching her system of grief resilience to anyone facing adversity.

Ruth holds a Master's Degree in Social Work from Loyola University Chicago. She also is a Licensed Clinical Social Worker in Illinois. At her private psychotherapy practice in Northfield, IL, she is honored to work with adolescents, adults, and families.

In addition to writing, Ruth enjoys nature hikes, movies, and laughing with her husband Alan. She also loves sharing meals with friends and family. Her greatest joy is spending time with her grandchildren and delighting in their growth.

For more information about Ruth E. Field, LCSW, please visit her website at www.GriefHelper.com.